The Love of Spirit

MY JOURNEY INTO MEDIUMSHIP

LEANDA RAE

Copyright © 2017 by Leanda Rae

The author of this book does not dispense medical advice or prescribe the use of any technique as a form of treatment for physical, medical or psychological problems or conditions. The intent of the author is only to offer information of a general nature for your general interest to help you in your quest for spiritual and emotional well-being. See your physician or health professional if you have a medical condition or are in need of mental health support. In the event you choose to use any of the techniques or suggestions in this book, the author and the publisher assume no responsibility for your actions.

Edited by: Elizabeth Duncan
Back Cover Photo: ©Dyana Soikie 2017

ISBN: 0987915703
ISBN-13: 978-0987915702

Dedication

For my daughters, with all my mighty love. For Gini, whose purple light will always shine. For all of you that have asked me where to begin, I hope this book will help you find your way. And for all of you that have been waiting decades for me to get this in print, thank you for waiting.

Contents

Acknowledgements

I am so thankful for the love from Spirit; all my spirit helpers, angels, guides, and all those working from the "unseen" realms for inspiring me, teaching me, bringing miracles and their humor, nudging me along, and showing me the expanse of their view and their love, for all of us.

Great thanks and gratitude for my sister, Elizabeth. Her skillful editing has brought decades of experiences into order and now to you, in this book. She has inspired me with her unique and ingenious morsels of insight.

Heartfelt thanks to all my clients and students, for your trust in me, and for inviting me to be a part of your journey. Thank you for allowing me to share my experiences with your loved ones, in this book. I am blessed to have you in my life.

XO, Leanda

Introduction

Throughout the years I've met hundreds of people that have asked me how I became a psychic medium. Did I just "know" I was a medium, could I always "do it" and the most frequently asked question, "How do I begin?"

Within these pages you will find the how, why and what, of my journey into mediumship and working with spirit. It's a world of angels, spirit guides, spirit animals, loved ones in spirit and miracles. You will also find two helpful exercises to start you off on your own discovery and further development of your psychic senses. You already use your intuitive senses—but maybe it's time to acknowledge and answer the nudge or inner calling from your own soul, and your ethereal helpers, to expand those inherent abilities.

Within this book I hope you find the answers that end any fear, the beginning of a great adventure, and the wonderful love of Spirit that is for, and with, you. The information that comes through to us is meant to provide us with hope, healing, inspiration, happiness and empowerment so we may live our lives to their fullest, now, knowing we have tremendous love and support from all that is Spirit.

CHAPTER 1

Spooked

I still recall, quite clearly, my first sighting of what I now know was the presence of Spirit. It was unknown and terrifying so I did what any kid would do: I closed my eyes.

Six was a momentous age for me because I became aware of myself in the world, within my family and with other people. I began to sense. It was also the year I became aware of the not-so-pretty side of life and relationships. But aside from being a kid and all the things that kids experience, I also saw ghostly things.

The house where I grew up had a long hallway that ran in front of three bedrooms; my parents had the big bedroom. On the other side of the hall (facing the big bedroom) was an open alcove where we hung our coats.

The alcove did not have a light but the hallway did, and that light was turned off. One evening as I walked down the hallway, I felt...jittery. I slowed down as I approached the alcove. I could see a very thin ribbon of mist about as tall as a person—but it was almost transparent. Instantly afraid, I closed my eyes and rushed into my parents' bedroom. I never told anyone that I had seen a ghostly ribbon. Even at six years of age, I felt no one would believe me or maybe they would call me a "nervous ninny", as I was sometimes called.

I successfully blocked out and avoided seeing any more misty materializations in closets. All of my time was dedicated to dance classes, going to school and growing up. I still had a fear of the dark and, like many children, I was creeped out by basements and dark attics. I was too young to know about spirit and energies and sensitivity.

***

The pivotal event—that wakeup call from Spirit—occurred when I was twelve years old. It was a difficult, beautiful experience that frightened me only because of the physical distress, not because of my contact with Spirit.

It was summer, it was hot and my friends and I wanted to go for a swim. The water in the local quarry was over thirty feet deep, easy to reach and best of all, free to use. We walked into the cold green water and started to swim across to the other side. I was nervous because I was a poor swimmer (and asthmatic). But there was a big St. Bernard dog swimming near me; maybe he could rescue me if I needed help. I remember this so clearly:

> *I am trying to be brave but suddenly I'm gasping for air and the dog is swimming away!*

I try to yell and wave my hand for help but I can't breathe. What should I do? If I kick to raise my arm high, I'll immediately sink into thirty feet of water. If I try to tread water, I'll suffocate anyway because my lungs just won't expand! This was a dumb idea.

> *I am up "here" now, quite peaceful. I can see myself far below, flailing in the dark quarry water. No-one knows I'm drowning, not even the dog. But "here" is a beautiful place, a peach-pink color everywhere. I feel no fear, no distress, only expansive, effortless peace and enduring love. Then a voice from somewhere asks me, "Do you want to stay or go back?"*

Instantly, without explanation, I remember. A feeling of deep love awakens within me when I hear the familiar voice. I have no name for that voice, only that I know it, and it does feel like "home". I remember how very old my soul is, how much wisdom I have gathered and that I have a LOT of work to do in this lifetime as a wise one, messenger for Spirit, healer, and teacher.

In fact, I say exactly that to the voice that surrounds me, "I have to go back; I have too much work to do." I don't hesitate to reply—it comes forth spontaneously. I just know that is my responsibility. I also know that the sheer amount of wisdom and knowledge in the Spirit realm can, and does, fill the universe.

As soon as that thought-sentence was out, I found myself back in my body, floundering and suffocating in cold green water, but substantially closer to the shore. I'm not sure how it all happened but I raised my hand out of the water, and someone waded in and pulled me out. I sat on a rocky shelf feeling nauseated and catching my breath. I was acutely aware of the lack of bliss as I sat on a hard rock in this reality.

I never told anyone about the event until I was almost 20 years old and the family started talking openly about paranormal experiences. It turns out that all the women on mother's side: my grandmother, my aunt and my mother, my sisters (and my brother) too, had experienced visions and precognition! I began to grasp the full depth of what my mother used to call her "dreams", which were really her own mediumistic communications with the spirit world.

***

When I was 15 years old, I had a verifiable and polite visitor from the spirit world. This was the start of my education in mediumship and spirit communication.

At that time, my bedroom was in the basement and a short walk away from the recreation room and TV area. That night I woke up around 4 a.m. with the sense that someone was standing in my bedroom doorway. I opened my eyes and saw a man in an army uniform looking at me. I was pretty sleepy so I couldn't figure out why my father, long retired from the military, would be wearing his uniform in the middle of the night. I snapped awake when I realized that the visitor was silently telling me that he was my father's friend and that he was no longer alive.

The spirit visitor never moved from the doorway. He was not scary or ghostly-looking but my fear took over as soon as I realized what was happening. I yanked the covers up over my head and stayed there until the sun came up! And as usual, I didn't mention it to anyone. Later that day, when my father returned from work, I heard him tell my mother that an old army buddy had died the previous night. I almost convinced myself that it was a dream, but I also began to sleep with a light on, hoping that I wouldn't wake up to another spirit standing in my bedroom door.

That's just what they did, these polite spirit visitors. They never did anything to frighten me. I did that all by myself. For many years, any spirit wanting to get my attention would politely stand in my bedroom doorway, waiting until I opened my eyes and acknowledged their presence. Only then would the spirit "download" a message and I would suddenly know what the spirit was saying, or impressing upon me.

Time went on and the polite visitors from the other side continued to randomly appear in my bedroom doorway at night. I did a lot of pacing and fretting about how to tell people about the messages I received. I began to dig into books on mediumship and psychic abilities, searching for the piece of information that would explain to me exactly what my gift was—or if I was just crazy. I had some curious experiences which left me shaking my head many times and asking, "Was that real?" I got married and had two babies. When I was 24 years old, the traffic in my bedroom doorway and all things psychic began to increase. For so many years I had been able to sit on my abilities, squash the extra senses—to a point. But then the calling came from Spirit, and my clairvoyance went into overdrive.

CHAPTER 2

What Do I Do?

There was never any plan to develop or pursue any kind of psychic study. As far as I was concerned, my intuition was kind of normal. My spirit visitors were intriguing but unsettling. Clairvoyance, mediumship and psychic ability were known to run in our maternal side of the family but they were never discussed.

I was now very busy working, having children, and moving several times—all those things that fill up the days and years. The spirit visitors were quiet for a long time and I believe it was because I was so busy. But once we settled into a permanent home and both children were sleeping through the night, the night-time doorway visits started up again. I began keeping track of those visitors even though it was happening infrequently. I wanted a record so I could try to make sense of their visits. Why were they still coming to me?

I had no user manual for my experiences, no mentor or teacher. The spirit people never spoke to me: I could only see them and describe what they looked like and take note of their clothing. Very rarely did a spirit person give me information telepathically (instant knowledge) about who they were connected or related to. But I had figured out that eventually someone connected to that spirit would cross my path.

One night I awoke to see a handsome young man standing in the doorway, wearing a very distinctive checked shirt. He had a smile on his face and I felt a sense of, "I'm fine, happy and relaxed". I acknowledged him and mentally said, "Hello" and then he left. Three days later I was looking out my living room window and I saw a young man walking up the driveway to my neighbor's house. He was a wearing the same distinctive checked shirt that my spirit visitor had been wearing—and I had my link from the spirit to this person! I waited impatiently until the young man left my neighbor's house. Then I went right over and knocked on the door.

My neighbor told me that the young man who visited him was his nephew. Three days earlier, his nephew's best friend had died in a car accident. I described the young spirit man who had visited me and my neighbor confirmed that the best friend who died was just as I described. That experience taught me that Spirit was intelligent enough to provide me, the medium-in-training, with ways to connect the dots and link a spirit visit to a living person so I could deliver a message. And in this case, this young spirit wanted to tell his best friend that he was safe and happy.

Sometimes my bedroom door visitors were connected to strangers I had not even met. But Spirit had a way to put me in the right place, whether it was the lady that stopped to talk with me on the side of the road (whose husband had briefly appeared in my doorway a few days prior) or the man in the local bar that just happened to take a seat at my table (whose aunt in spirit visited to show her support). In my experience, Spirit does find a way to connect the dots wherever possible.

***

The turning point—when I dedicated myself to training—occurred when two spirit people, both victims of homicide, contacted me. The victim of an unknown killer made herself known to me one day while I was watching the news.

I was making dinner for our family; the television was on in the living room while I cooked. For several days, the news channel reports had mentioned a young lady who was missing. That night they showed her picture again and asked for help to locate her. I happened to sit down for a moment in front of the TV as the story and her picture were displayed. I clearly remember the moment like it was in slow motion: I blinked and before my eyes appeared an old style Polaroid® photograph. In that blink I knew:

> *"I can see the road where she is laying. I see the trees, the gravel shoulders, and the grass. I know this road ends at water. And I know she is dead."*

The experience caught me completely by surprise. I said to my husband, "Honey, I think I've just had a 'Kodak' moment."

That vision created a huge level of anxiety in me. I could clearly see the place where she was but I did not get the name of the road! I paced in circles wondering if I should be telling police what I saw. But how could I when all I could say was "the road ended at water"? The location was hundreds of miles away and its roadways were expansive and unknown to me. Plus—I would sound like one of those off-the-wall psychics if I called to report a clairvoyant vision.

That night I tried again and again to connect with her spirit so that I could get a road name, but I had no success. Within 48 hours of my vision, police did find her body and it was, sadly, just as she showed me. I felt very discouraged; I felt like I had failed her. I was frustrated because I could see so much detail and I knew without doubt that her body was there. But where "there" was— the name of that road—didn't come through. It was a very long time before I learned that perhaps I did not get the road's name because she didn't know it either. Her killer was eventually caught and jailed for life.

About a week later, I had a second clairvoyant vision, a "movie" this time. That day I was doing household chores with the TV on in the background; there was a report of a missing child. She had disappeared from within her apartment building, and the search was on for her. Having two young children of my own, my heart went out to the desperate mother and I wished that I could do something to help. There were no messages from Spirit.

However, the "movie" began later that day as I sat resting, not really focusing on anything. Suddenly, like being awake in a dream, I found myself standing on the rooftop of that apartment building—the one from the news story about the missing child. I could see everything clearly, especially colors. I saw the city spread out below; the whole scene seemed flooded with sunlight. I saw a small girl standing not too far away from me. Her back was to me so I couldn't see her face. She was looking out over the side of the roof, just standing still.

It was as if I was suddenly transported hundreds of miles away to the top of that building. I could see her hair moving in the breeze. Then a wave of energy came over me and it became a persistent internal "push". I heard, "At the top. I'm at the top. At the top. At the top." Push, push, push. The thought became filled with an intensity almost like anxiety. Even now, I can easily remember and feel the insistence of this spirit pushing her message through to me. I shook my head and was back in my living room.

Once again I began to walk in circles. Why was I receiving this information? Should I call the police? Would they believe me? They had combed that apartment building from top to bottom, including the rooftop, and they had not found her. But still her message was pushing at me. At the top, at the top, at the top. I couldn't get it out of my thoughts. I was so torn. How could I explain that I knew she was dead?

When they finally did locate her body, she was right where she had told me she would be found—at the top. We eventually learned that she had been moved from the rooftop before the first search of that area. Her body was then returned to the rooftop, and the police found her after another search. Once they located her, the "push" of her message stopped. I was filled with sadness for her family and guilt for not being brave enough to call someone about my vision. I felt amazed that she and the previous young lady—those two souls—had communicated with me. Yet I felt so inadequate because I didn't know how to get more information and details.

I knew that I needed an expert, a psychic, a mentor or medium, to help me know what to do next. A deep sense of responsibility began to rise within me. Why, after all this time, was I suddenly getting messages from these two young victims of violence? I truly felt compelled to do more—I felt the call to mediumship. It was time to act; there was no more avoiding what I had always known. I was psychic, clairvoyant and a medium. I had a job to do and it was as a messenger for Spirit. I had to find help.

I searched for a psychic in and around the small town where I lived. Fortunately, I found a local psychic with a good reputation so I made an appointment to see her. Judy had a reputation as a very down-to-earth mystic. I will always consider her to be my first mentor and one of my most important influences. She was a lovely woman, mother, grandmother with a direct, straightforward approach and an air of mystery. She was the person that helped me learn a few basic but very important concepts that I still teach and pass on to my clients and workshop participants. Sadly, she passed away unexpectedly and even though I was no longer in contact with her at that time, she still gets the credit for being the person that started me off on the right foot.

***

I was relieved to finally connect with a professional but at the same time I was nervous to ask for help. I wasn't quite sure what I was supposed to be asking. I gave Judy the details of my experiences starting with the two most recent homicide victims. I asked her, "Why did I have those visions of where the bodies were? And why do spirits stand in my bedroom doorway when I'm sleeping?"

Judy asked me to "read" her; after that, she seemed satisfied that I was speaking the truth and that I really was clairvoyant. She suggested that I was now at a decision point in my life. I could either continue to run away from my intuitive abilities and the night visitors, or I could embrace my abilities in the daytime hours and learn more about them. She made it clear that the spirit world had already made up its mind about me and wanted to work with me. Her statement did ring true again a few years later. An elder shaman that I was visiting explained to me that my soul had already accepted the "job" as healer long before I was born. He was not at all surprised to hear of my connection with Spirit.

Judy was one of the first people in my life to tell me that I should embrace my "job". That was HUGE. Up to that point, I had never had confirmation of my ability from anyone besides my own mother; I certainly had no clue that there was a choice in the matter. And with that first meeting my education began.

That day, Judy explained that it was clear the spirit world knew I was a medium. It was up to me how I wanted to handle that relationship now. Judy advised me that if I chose not to embrace my mediumship, most likely I would continue to have the doorway visitors. At the very least, I would be able to shelve it for a while, but Spirit would eventually want to get my attention again. I had to make a choice. Did I embrace this or continue to be confused and reluctant?

How could I refuse to learn more? I chose to embrace the "job". Judy began to help me understand how to work with my abilities, with the ethereal realms. It was from her that I learned about the "contract" with Spirit that I needed to put in place. Essentially, I needed to set some boundaries that worked for both the spirit world communicators and me.

She then provided some very helpful advice and it got me started on the first steps to fine-tuning my senses. Since then I have learned what works and doesn't work for me. What works for you may be different. I have learned that there are some basic rules when working with these cosmic energies. They are good rules and guidelines that exist to preserve your well-being and the well-being of the spirit world. I have learned much from all my teachers and others in my field, but mostly I have gained the largest knowledge and skill from my own trial-and-error processes, from experimenting and learning with Spirit, and just by doing the work.

One of the first things I learned was to "slow it down". By "it" I mean the clairvoyant images, movies and words. Now that I was aware of these psychic impressions, I was also acutely aware of the speed at which they would zip across my forehead. Although it's a process that is happening in my mind, it feels like they are actually sweeping across the inside of my forehead like a ticker tape roll, from left to right. Some might call that the "mind's eye". For me, it was a highway with bits of words and images moving at highway speed. It often felt like a chattering brain in constant motion.

The very first exercise I was given was designed to help me pay more attention to an image or impression as it was happening. If I was slow to realize that a clairvoyant image or message was travelling across my mind's eye, I could still have success if I acknowledged that I was sensing a message or image. This was the most important lesson.

Acknowledging the receipt of a psychic message is the response that Spirit must have from you in order for Spirit to send you more messages! This acknowledgement tells the universe that you are paying attention, even if the message zips by too fast for you to catch, and even if you don't know what you're supposed to do next. It will then send you more information, more psychic bits and pieces, more sensations and more spirit communications. You do not have to be a professional anything to do this. You just have to pay attention and then tell Spirit, "Thanks, I got that."

Training then became learning about my personal style of receiving information. I also found tools—energy training, modalities and methods— that enhanced and helped focus my sensing ability. Good communication skills were important, and I studied and practiced these skills every day.

Once I began to pay attention and acknowledge the psychic information that was coming at me, I started to get more information more frequently. I practiced mentally grabbing the tail of a fleeting image or word before it zipped out of my "mind's eye". Then I would imagine myself pulling it back towards me until it was right in front of my "eye" again. It took only a few days for the ticker-tape of images to slow down, once I started to pay attention and acknowledge that I'd received something. Once things slowed down I was able to understand what the psychic impressions and images were trying to tell me.

The next step in my beginner shoes was to act on the messages received. This was Judy's second piece of advice. Acting on a message—whether telling someone you have a message or taking the next left turn—also signals that you are listening. It strengthens your acknowledgement to Spirit that you are listening, aware and ready to act on that divine guidance. I've always felt rather shy about spouting off-the-cuff to strangers about what I've seen, so I made choices about when and to whom I would divulge psychic messages.

Tact and discernment are a priority when approaching both friends and strangers. You won't find me walking up to people in grocery stores or the checkout line and delivering messages. If I am meant to give a complete stranger a message, then I wait for Spirit to arrange things so that person approaches me first. Tact, discretion and compassion have to be a part of your skill set.

The third wise piece of advice that my first mentor gave me was to set up my "contract" with the spirit world. It was very exciting to be working with Spirit and all metaphysical energies but I also had a young family and worked a full time job. There had to be some balance. As much as I was both fascinated and freaked out about my night-time visitors, I also wanted some level of control. I was just learning to develop my abilities and gain an understanding of what I was doing! So boundaries were and still are important. I agreed to work with Spirit during the daytime hours—to be available for them and dedicate myself to paying attention and developing. In return, they (the spirit people) could no longer wake me up at night.

That's it. That's all the contract was. I had taken a few days to think about how to word the contract and also to look within myself to see if this was truly the path I wanted to go down. Since I was really feeling the call to work in this way, the decision was not difficult. I hoped that this simple contract would, in fact, end my polite night-time company. It did. The effect was immediate. The day I made my commitment to my contract, the night time awakenings stopped. I thought that was quite incredible.

Of course because I am kind of a skeptic and like to prove things to myself I would eventually test that contract.

CHAPTER 3

New Teachers, New Skills

Along my way I did some studying in Shamanic healing techniques such as rattling and drumming. Because I've always had a sense of being closely linked to trees, I learned about the healing properties of trees and began to incorporate the techniques I was learning into my intuitive practice. My mentor presented me with a raven feather just before we stopped our regular meetings, and I cherished the gift. At the time she told me that a shaman had gifted it to her and when the time was right, she would pass it to the next healer that was to carry it. The feather became a part of my daily meditative and prayer time, and when the time was right, many years later, I then passed it to one of my students who was ready to follow her own path as a healer.

Little did I know that the next gift to arrive would have such a special purpose and place in my work as a healer. A beautiful feather for me to hold and a healer in spirit that I came to know as "Grandfather" arrived within hours of each other one day. "Grandfather" taught me how to use the new healing feather during energy sessions and would direct me to areas of the body that needed healing or adjusting of energy. He is just one of the spirit healers that I have been blessed to have teach me and guide me as he brings his healing to others.

***

My focus and desire to learn about my sensitivity to energy led me to study Reiki. When I learned the practice of Reiki and experienced its energy and benefit, I found that it was a perfect match for me as it helped me own all my extra-senses and open them more fully. I learned to listen to the energy in a room, to listen to the vibrations and energy of my client receiving Reiki, to sense all the energies and to trust and follow the guidance of those energies. I learned to trust as I came to know the energies of not only my spirit team, but also my healing team and my client's healing team. As one huge sensing exercise, Reiki was like a permission slip for me to speak about what I was sensing.

I studied palmistry as well but soon discovered that instead of reading the palm lines as traditional palm readers do, I would see images on the palms. I studied tarot as well, and also discovered when I tried to follow the "book" method of reading the cards for others, my clairvoyance and clairsentience always stepped up and presented images or knowledge and sensations beyond any technical card meaning. I even studied reflexology and became certified so that I had another modality behind which I could hide my true ability.

As with all the other methods, information would flow to me about each client. Spirit visitors and guides would also arrive for both types of sessions, and often I was guided by them (and by Grandfather) during healing sessions. I slowly began to trust my own personal method of receiving information. I also recognized that palm reading, tarot cards, runes and Reiki were simply tools to help me focus and be open to the energies and presences that are there. The tools weren't giving me the details. That was coming from the psychic airwaves, my own energy body, and from those in the spiritual realms. Still, I was not putting any focus on mediumship because I did not know how to do that.

When I felt confident enough to take my intuitive abilities and services out to the public, I began to offer readings. During some sessions, but not all, a spirit person would appear to me. Just as my childhood visitors stood silently in my bedroom door, this spirit person would stand silently and impress a message upon me. It was not until later when I took some mediumship training that I learned ways to identify who the spirit person was, and how to identify that person's role in the client's life—whether it was dad or mom, grandmother or aunt. Until I took that training, I could only provide a description of the spirit person and the message that was sent.

Until I had further training, I did not know that I could ask a spirit for a name. I really did not think I could possibly get this level of detail. I was particularly frustrated one day not being able to figure out how to get place names from a spirit. I said out loud with lots of exasperation, "Come ON! At least give me the first letter of the name!" Sure enough, the very next contact a spirit person made (who was also a victim of homicide) came with great details and images of their resting spot, and a letter "C". Spirit gave me exactly what I asked for—the first letter (which turned out to be correct along with all the other details provided).

I was now learning that it was important to be more specific with my requests. I wasted no time in asking for names but it took me a while longer to start to receive complete names. But first letters I could now get! I know it is possible to get whatever the spirit communicator wants to give and is able to give; from names and dates to a favorite food. I also know that it's up to me to listen well to the information being provided.

It's not always the medium's ability that affects how well information from someone in spirit is received. Sometimes the spirit person needs practice too.

Sometimes, it's not my place to say anything. Spirit knows if a person is not ready or able to receive the information. And sometimes, the medium needs to be less nervous and simply trust the process.

***

As I slowly began to figure out how my psychic and mediumship ability worked, I began to piece together something called my "glossary". My glossary is best described as "this means that". If I clairvoyantly see a car tire with chains wrapped around it, I know it means the person sitting with me feels like either the job is a grind, or that he or she is grinding and toiling away, dragging at something. If I see flowing water, it means the person with me is experiencing huge change and shifts in life, and he or she feels unable to find steady footing. For some, a red rose means the spirit person is extending his or her love. Pink roses mean the spirit person is sending birthday greetings. So my glossary is very personal, for the spirit communicators are using what is already in my mind as their catalogue for the glossary.

In the beginning of my study, my glossary was being built quickly. I found it very fascinating to learn how the images I knew were used for meanings for a spirit to communicate. After years of training and experience, my glossary does not get used as heavily since I am now able to hear and see the information much more directly, but my glossary is still being built. The more I read and learn on all other subjects, whether I am travelling or learning geography or a new language, the spirit communicators will know I have that information and they can use it to express their thoughts and feelings.

***

I attended a mediumship workshop taught by Doreen Virtue, PhD, the author and creator of Angel Therapy®. There I started to learn how I could identify a spirit person and the spirit's relationship to a client, using a handy diagram. I began to piece together the new knowledge from that workshop with the experiences I had already been having with my spirit communicators. Once this workshop was finished, I returned home filled with a new confidence in my new knowledge. In turn, I found my link with the spirit world strengthened. I began to dedicate more time to offering sessions to the public.

Healing Touch® and Lomilomi Hawaiian massage were then studied and added to my list of modalities. My understanding of my clairsentience and sensitivity to all kinds of energies expanded. Angels were suddenly tapping me on the shoulder calling for my attention so I also trained and was certified as an Angel Therapy Practitioner®.

Although I no longer need to use the particular tool I learned during my first mediumship workshop, it was such a valuable method for me at that stage of my learning that I often share it with beginning students. This and other handy tools and methods are aids and I stress that all these tools are just that: assistive aids to help build confidence, knowledge, focus and consistency in a developing student. Once experienced enough, and with practice, these tools aren't necessary as you discover your personal style of working and gain trust in your ability and your spiritual helpers. You will be able to express all psychic and spirit communication and details as they arrive, whether through clairvoyance (seeing), clairsentience (feeling/sensing), claircognizance (knowing), clairaudience (hearing), clairscent (smell, also called clairalience) or clairgustance (taste).

All this training helped me to intimately know my senses and how I received psychic, energetic and spiritual information. It helped me to build my personal glossary and as I learned from one workshop, I would then learn something new from Spirit, angels, and spirit guides. I am still learning and I love to gain new and different insights, and of course, practice!

***

Development Tip

Once we learn a lesson or have an experience—something that brings us new knowledge or a new viewpoint—Spirit will use that new knowledge to communicate and connect in ways we couldn't have done before.

CHAPTER 4

Learning About Angels

When I started my spiritual and intuitive development, angels did not fit into my plan. I was going to be a grounded and no-nonsense healer, firmly entrenched in the earth's energies and mysteries. My tools would be stones and crystals, rattles and drums. As far as I was concerned, Angels were for people who had a higher connection or who needed life-saving help.

I found my way to the angels through a friend who suggested that I read a book written by Doreen Virtue, PhD. It seems that there are two ways to fall into the presence of angels: either you have some childhood feeling or knowledge of them that you cherish, or you are led to them in a way that makes you very aware of their presence and activity. I am so happy that I was led to the angels. I have had my life transformed, and the miracles that I have experienced reassure me and confirm that angels are with me, always. They are always here, just waiting to be invited into our lives.

If you want to begin communication with angels all you have to do is invite them in to your life. It is that easy. You can say out loud or in your thoughts, "Angels, I invite you to communicate with me daily, and be present in my life daily."

If you need confirmation that they are around, or that they have heard you, simply ask, "Angels, please give me clear confirmation that you are with me, in a manner that I will know the confirmation is from you."

If you think you are not hearing, seeing, sensing or receiving confirmation, try to begin a regular practice of meditation. Making your mind quiet, even for five minutes a day; this gives them space to communicate. If you are anything like me, your mind chatters away constantly and leaves no room for communication from the celestial world. Then you lie in bed at night wondering why you haven't heard from your angels or your guides. Don't be discouraged—they are there, and most likely are waiting patiently for the opportunity to be heard.

Once you get used to opening that quiet space in your thoughts, you will find that it gets easier to listen for celestial guidance. And, if you are anything like me, you will get a confirmation but won't believe it! So it's ok to ask for three confirmations from your angels—three signs that will leave you with no doubt that they are communicating with you.

The popular writings of many people that work with angels state that angels will use print (newspapers, magazines), synchronicity, words, television, dreams, timing, chance meetings (again, synchronicity), to communicate with you. I agree and I have experienced all those things. Angels can and often do speak the loudest in the most subtle ways.

***

I have completed many angel readings for my clients and I find that every person does most certainly have at least one angel who is a guardian—hence the term guardian angel. But each person has multiple angels, sometimes for different things, for different times in our lives. For those people who have not asked their angels into their lives, or for those who have told them, "Get lost!", their angels are still standing about eight feet from them, patiently waiting for the instant that they are invited in to help.

Angels appear to me in a number of ways. I clairvoyantly "see" them as brilliant streams or columns of moving light and energy, and as sparkling balls of light. Some are hugely tall and some are very small. They also appear in the classic artist rendition of human-looking beings with large, feathery wings, sometimes appearing in long flowing white robes. When they appear to me as the "classic" winged angel, I usually do not see a face because angels really have no faces, but they will present themselves to us in whatever form we will best perceive them. That means when I am reading for a client, and angels appear as beautiful beings in long flowing white robes with expansive wing sets, I know that the person I am reading for will perceive them best that way. For some people, that is a safe way to imagine or receive a clear mental image of their angels. I know that in my first experiences I was quite happy to see one of my angels with those famous wings! I also know that when I am working with someone who is farther along in understanding the spirit realm and energy beings, the angels appear more in what I feel is their true form—as streams of energy and light.

Angels also come with sound, which is actually their vibration. Some individuals (including me) can perceive these sounds. Sometimes a client will ask me for an angel's name and I respond with a sound **like** the sound I hear from that angel. It does not take the form of a name as we know it. You can call your angels any names you want, but their true essence as energy, light and sound/vibration is such that we humans probably could not pronounce those sounds. However, for those individuals that require a clearer mental image of an angel, often a name will be given—and it is understandable. That is why you may leave an angel reading being told that your angels' names are something like Peter, Solonar, Benna, Aguel, or David. And sometimes you may leave having been told that the angel's name is like a sound, and I will make the sound to the best of my ability.

When I ask the angels what else they want to say for this book, they tell me that people need to listen. Just listen. To be successful in listening to your angels you have to trust yourself, your intuition, and be still inside. Chatter that rolls rampant in your mind will certainly stomp out the voice of your angels, as will anxiety, anger and stubbornness held within yourself. Angels want to communicate with us. They have the ability to have the biggest voice.

You need to know that they love you, every bit of your essence and being; they see and know your light within. They wait patiently and sometimes excitedly for you to first believe, then acknowledge and then invite them into your life. They love you no matter how rotten your day is, or how crabby you are. They are the comfort in a dark night and their sense of humor really makes me realize that we take ourselves much too seriously!

***

I have been involved in many discussions with people about whether angels are angelic beings from heaven or whether they are all "Spirit". Some feel that all our ethereal helpers are the souls of people that have passed on. Some feel there is a hierarchy in the ethereal realms, and Archangels and Angels have never lived life as a human, and never will. Are our spiritual helpers highly evolved souls, or the task force of the heavens, or beings from different dimensions? All I know is what I have experienced, what others have shared with me from their experiences, and how these experiences have helped me discover things that are truly amazing and inspiring.

I have felt the energies of many angels to whom we have given names. They all **feel** different energetically, to me; they think differently from each other and have different frequencies of vibration and light. I can perceive (much the same way I receive details from a loved one in spirit) how evolved, experienced, wise, authoritative, and determined each angel is. I can sense the weight of their mission and message. They are all loving. Some are more serious and some more light-hearted, but all of them love all of us.

My Angel Josephine

The first time I recognized an angel in my meditations was when I met Josephine. During one of my meditations, this lovely angel appeared to me; she made it clear that she was there specifically for me. With her youthful energy and lightness that seemed to sing to me, the name Josephine just popped into my head.

She appeared to me as female in her early twenties, with long wavy light red hair and wearing a floor-length cream-white gown. (As mentioned earlier, I was happy to have this somewhat traditional angel vision—gown, wings—long before I had more exposure and experiences.) Josephine seemed to move very quickly, and she would send her thoughts to me so fast that I had a hard time catching up mentally, so I would just clairvoyantly hitch a ride with her and let her fly me to whatever she wanted me to see. The first time that Josephine appeared, she said that she had something to show me, and off we went. In my vision we floated at night over what looked like a small mountain range, and in the valley below I could see a large airplane, crashed. Red and orange fires dotted the dark.

I said, "Why do you want me to see this? It's really depressing."

She said, "I want you to see the grey."

Then she disappeared from my sight and suddenly my meditation was over. I opened my eyes and said, "What the heck was **that**?" I really had to think about why I was shown this vision; what did it mean? It finally made sense when I realized that it was a high impact vision because **that** was what I wanted! I was like many people, I wanted there to be no doubt that I had seen an angel or experienced something psychic. I looked for that earth-shaking vision and Josephine had provided one to get my attention.

Josephine's statement "I want you to see the grey", also puzzled me for a long time. Eventually, Josephine and Spirit provided another lesson, and from that I learned what that "grey" really was, and how I might be a creator and builder of it.

Despite being puzzled by the grand meaning of this initial vision with Josephine, I found that if I was patient and waited, the clarity would come and find me. One other piece to this vision clicked when I participated in a past life regression that same year, where I discovered my own history with airplanes.

Josephine was a constant companion to me for about three years and I valued her presence greatly. She became part of my daily life and it was wonderful to have her with me. Within one week of having angel Josephine enter my life, I walked into a store looking for an angel statue. It didn't take long to find. I walked to the first aisle, looked up and there on the top shelf was— Josephine! Or rather, a statue of what she looked like in my visions of her. Of course I bought it. That statue traveled with me across the country a few times until I realized that I either had to travel less or leave the statue at home. I asked one of my sisters to "babysit" her but really I asked Josephine to watch over her too. I was feeling sad and apologizing to Josephine the statue for leaving her behind when my clairaudient ear heard Josephine say, "You are talking to a statue." I burst out laughing because she was right; Josephine was NOT in the statue. I connected with the statue because it reminded me of her and her energy, but Josephine the angel was not bound or encapsulated inside that statue. Feeling sheepish, I immediately "let go" of the stone angel.

No matter how much attachment we put on statues, photos, trinkets or papers of angels and Archangels, they don't really live in these things. These items are just tools to help us focus and connect with the angel realm.

I know Josephine is always around to help, but her role with me has changed over the years and now I see her only in times when her special gifts are needed for something I am trying to accomplish or learn. She also assists me with client readings and consultations, adding her input and guidance where required. Josephine is the angel that helped me to know that angels are not only providers of divine guidance, love and light but they are also trusted friends. I know that Josephine, the angels and Archangels will arrive when asked or when needed. They are always there.

CHAPTER 5

Angelic Encounters

When an angel walks into my day it's always memorable. From miracles that save lives to the stranger that lends a hand – it's always very special and I feel so blessed to have been in their presence. Let me introduce you to a few of the angels I have met along my way.

The Guardian

I met a guardian angel long before I ever picked up a book about angels. I didn't ask to meet one, it just happened, and he was beautiful.

Years ago when I was married, my brother-in-law and his wife were expecting twins. Early in the third trimester of the pregnancy, his wife was urgently sent to the hospital because the babies were in serious trouble. One baby was "sitting" on top of the other, and the twin on the bottom was fighting to survive. An early delivery was not possible because the babies were too young.

One night, while my sister-in-law was in hospital, I was asleep in my bed when I felt someone sit down beside me. I opened my eyes, looked up and saw the most beautiful young man. He looked to be about twenty years old, with beautiful black hair. He was very clean and neatly dressed. He smiled and looked at me, and I felt complete purity, love and joy. He was the complete, whole, total encompassing love and peacefulness you would expect from the most perfect being in the universe. It was so much I could feel my mind trying to grasp the largeness of his purity and truth. He spoke to me without words, telling me that one of the babies had died and that he would be the baby's guardian on the other side. The angel made it clear that he was not the baby's soul visiting, as some might think. Instead of feeling sad, I felt joyful because my nephew was going to be with this angel on the other side. This rush of joy made me sit up; as soon as I did, the angel vanished. I was so excited that I turned to my sleeping husband and yelled, "Wow, you'll never guess who I just met!" He really wasn't that thrilled because it was 4 a.m. But I was excited because I had just met pure love.

Later that day we learned that baby Adam had indeed died in the early hours of the morning. I felt blessed to know that baby was already carried, loved and cared for on the other side by his beautiful guardian angel.

Santa Angel

Angels can take many forms and I still cherish the memory of the evening I met an angel in human form. I had spent the day giving Reiki treatments to people attending a Vancouver health expo. I was tired, but also feeling good about being able to participate as a healer at this event. Afterward my co-workers and I finished a hearty pub dinner and I headed home on the evening bus. The bus was almost empty; I sat down and glanced over at the other two passengers. One was an older woman; the other was an older man with white hair, a white beard and a belly. Dressed in jeans and a colorful shirt, he actually looked like Santa Claus on his day off. And he was whistling like a bird—**exactly** like a bird. It was as if the bus was full of canaries; it was amazing! The other woman turned around and said to this man, "You are doing a better job of song than the birds themselves."

He replied, "I can talk to the birds."

Well, now he had my full attention. He started to tell us of a bird that he had once brought back to life, and then he continued to whistle. There are no words to describe the clear and perfect sound that came from his whistling. It was a thirty-minute ride to my stop, which was the end of the bus route. I'm not sure how the bus driver was feeling, or even if he was paying much attention to us. If he had looked he would have seen two women with wide kid grins unable to stop smiling, sitting across from a Santa Claus lookalike who made the bus sound like it was full of bluebirds, robins and canaries.

The other woman disembarked a few stops before mine. When the bus made its final stop, I stood up to leave. I couldn't stop smiling, even in my thoughts. I stepped off the bus and the Santa lookalike stepped off behind me. I wanted to say something but no words came out, not even a thank-you. I could only smile and wave goodbye as he stood on the sidewalk smiling back at me.

I turned and began to walk down the street towards the house. A nagging feeling grew with every step I took. After twenty steps I stopped and turned around. I really felt that I had unfinished business with this man—I had to do something but I didn't know what. Santa was standing in the same spot, looking at me. I followed my intuition and walked back to him. I asked, "Have we met before?"

He replied, "Yes, I know all about you. You used to be a dancer." That statement certainly raised my eyebrows because it was true.

Then he said, "You have the energy. What do you do?" I told him that I had just come from the health expo and I had been doing Reiki.

He said, "Can I hold your hands?" I felt total trust, complete safety and no reason why I shouldn't let him hold my hands.

He took my hands, looked me square in the eyes and said, "Keep doing what you're doing. You have the healing energy, you have IT." Suddenly a rush of heat surged into my heart and chest and I was filled with warm love and a feeling of being completely protected and safe.

Somewhere deep within me I knew we had met before, and this was an angel standing with who knew me, knew my soul, and came to encourage me to continue on my path. The best way to describe the connection would be that our thoughts joined and the angel spoke to me, he also spoke within me, to my heart and mind about why he was there. I knew he was an angel.

He released my hands; I smiled and said, "Thank you."

I took two steps to leave and then I just had to hug him! The energy of this angel was so neutral, peaceful and true that I almost couldn't help myself. We hugged, and he then turned to go on his way, and I turned the opposite direction to go walk down the street again towards home. I walked about ten steps and turned around again—I had to see if he really was an angel. I rushed back to the bus stop but he was not there. I walked to the intersection where I could see for half a mile in each direction. I could not see him. He had vanished just as the angels from other encounters had disappeared. I hadn't asked for an angel, I hadn't been thinking of angels. The only thing I had done earlier in the day was question my choices about working as a healer. And it seems the angels sent me the form they thought I would find most comforting—Santa Claus.

The Moth Angel

At one point in my life I really wanted to see angels of every kind. New to working and connecting with angels, I began a daily routine of meditation, journaling, praying and chanting and tried to contain my frustration. I wanted to see an angel **now**! After about a week I felt miserable because I had no results.

One day, during the office lunch hour, I trudged outside to stand in an alcove of the building to get some fresh air. It was winter and very cold; the air was hinting of snow and I was missing my dad. He had passed away two years earlier, and sometimes when I was feeling blue I longed for his rare but wise insights about life.

My dad was in no way spiritual or religious. He had no use for anything that was not tangible, empirical or practical. As I stood in that cold alcove I thought to myself, "Ok, if ever there was a good time for me to see an angel now would be it!" This would be a good test because my dad would never (as far as I was concerned) communicate from spirit because he was never a believer.

Suddenly a small beige moth appeared near the sidewalk at the corner of the alcove. As it flittered around the corner in the wind, I wondered why a moth was out in this cold weather. I thought to myself, "Well, if this is an angel it will come straight to me." And that is exactly what it did. I watched in awe as this little moth flitted up and down, up and down and came directly to me and landed on my right shoulder. I was dumbstruck. I thought, "What do I do now?" So I just stood there, afraid to turn my head in case it took off. But I did look down at it, resting completely still on my shoulder. I asked if it had a message for me but got no response. I just stood there for a minute or two not knowing quite what to do.

So I thought, "Ok, angel, you got yourself in here (to the alcove). If you are really an angel you will just miraculously vanish!"

The little moth lifted off my shoulder and flitted up toward the alcove ceiling. Now this alcove had glass and concrete walls on three sides and a solid roof. The only way for this moth to get out was to leave the way it came in—out the entrance (which was about eight feet wide). As I watched, the moth floated up to the ceiling. No way out. I smugly thought that I would now be disappointed and this bubble of angel thoughts would soon be popped. Then, I blinked. The moth was gone. I searched the ceiling, the glass windows, the ground, everywhere to see if it was stuck anywhere. It was not. I checked outside the alcove but there was no way it could get by me without me seeing it. So in the blink of an eye it had vanished.

I don't know how that little moth angel disappeared but I do know that it was on an angelic mission for or on behalf of my dad. The angels had heard my thoughts and my call to them. Angels have the ability to utilize anything to make their presence known. They can appear in many different forms and will send butterflies, moths, birds, and lots of other creatures and objects as signs they are near.

Children, Angels and Fairies

After being introduced to the angels and having my encounters with Josephine, the Santa angel and the moth angel, I began to look for someone in the area that I could talk to about angels. Because I was new to the city, I did not know very many people so I asked my angels to guide me to someone that would be able to answer some of my questions. It did not take long before I happened upon a small advertisement posted on a wall in a market that said "Angel Meditations", with the name and contact info of the host.

Once you realize how incredibly talented the angels and the spirit helpers are at getting you where they want you to be, you will no longer question how things fall into place, and you'll just feel happy every time they do. So I was excited to be so quickly guided to this lady who hosted angel meditations. A few days later I was seated in this lady's living room chatting about my new experiences with angels, asking questions and preparing to for the angel meditation. The guided meditation was to take me through three stages of consciousness so that I could connect with the vibration and frequency of the angelic realm. New to the vibration of angels as I was, it was helpful to be guided through my chatty mind to a place of stillness and openness. Setting our intent for the meditation, we began.

Since I am strongly clairvoyant, I tend to have clear visuals. They become even clear when I am in an environment where it is safe to really let go and slip into an altered state of consciousness without worrying about any expectations or interruptions. As this was my first angel meditation, I had no expectations, only hope that I would be successful in connecting with the angelic realm. As I settled in and let the words of my host guide me gently I began my journey to the angelic realm.

In the beginning, all I had to do was imagine myself in an empty space, the starting point before walking towards each level of consciousness and vibration. Very quickly I saw myself walking, wearing a long white dress. The wind was blowing softly around me and my long white scarf fluttering behind me. I looked younger, and I saw that I had strawberry blond hair that was wrapped in a bun on top of my head. As I walked, I saw a set of small stairs. By the time I reached them I was fully "in" my vision, not just watching myself from the sidelines. Then, standing at the top of the short steps I looked out onto more open space, like viewing the countryside from atop a hill. My host guided me to ask for a guide or angel to visit, but there was no one there. All was beautiful and still. As I began to turn to start walking toward the next level of consciousness (as guided by my host), the head of a young man appeared. I thought to myself, "Wow, he looks like Prince Charming in my childhood storybooks." All I could see was his head, but I invited him to come to the next level with me.

Still guided by my host, I walked across the platform into nothingness and space with the intent that I was going to the second level of consciousness and a higher vibration. Now I found myself on another platform that had a sitting bench. As I stood on that platform, I began to see a woman in blue and many other beings, but only some of them fit my "everyday human" look. The woman/being wore everything blue: a tight fitting outfit with a cone shaped hat. I saw a person who also seemed to be an animal. He was zebra-striped, very bendable, and quite happy to be two different beings at the same time. There were many more and I could not remember them all. It was very different—or, **they** were different looking. But that was just fine. I felt joyful and safe in this journey.

My host instructed me to then continue on to the next level of consciousness and vibration. In my vision, I turned around and with a few steps found myself on the next platform, the third level. It too had a sitting bench that I sat upon and, following the guidance of my host, began to visualize a giant white candle. At the same time I asked for angels to appear to me. As I focused on the large flame of the big white candle I began to see shapes appear, transforming the flame of the candle until the candle itself disappeared and was replaced by the angels.

The first angel to appear had the traditional wings, as depicted in many drawings and paintings. Then a tall blue curtain began to appear and as it did, it started to shape itself into a long cape, made of many lengths of material. I knew that someone was coming into my visualization space, and in the next moment the cape parted and to my amazement angels started to pour out from inside the cape's opening. I saw one angel after another floating out from the cape, in a steady stream— all with different looks! Then the angels began to flow even faster from the cape. It was as if someone hit the high-speed button and all the angels were pouring out of the cape all at once! The faster the angels came forth, the more blue the cape became, becoming deep with the colors from periwinkle to water blue in the process. As amazing as this vision was, I did not expect what happened next.

Thousands of tiny angels and other small beings that looked like fairies came forth from the sides of the cape. Like a giant corps de ballet, there were gold and purple and sparkly angels and fairy-like beings streaming forth. I couldn't believe it—it was awesome. The entire time the angels were pouring forth, the tall blue cape began to grow even taller and take shape. I realized that there was a being wearing the cape and this being was **extremely** tall—much bigger than me. My jaw actually dropped at the size of this angel; even my host noticed, and after the meditation she asked what I had seen.

As this angel's appearance became clearer, I could see a woman with her head covered in the same blue material, like a hood. However her hood kept changing and moving as if it too were displaying the many features of this angel. Although her facial details were not clear, the energy and warmth she projected was of great love and of someone smiling broadly. I had to look a very long way up at her, for her height was about 8 or 10 feet. My awe of this beautiful being and her thousands of angels was so great and overwhelming that I wondered if I was going to fall on my knees. It never even crossed my mind that I was in a meditation for I was solidly in that place and living it.

Prior to beginning the meditation, my host had suggested I ask any questions I wanted to the angels that appeared—but all my questions had vanished in the presence of this great angel and the thousands of small and tiny angels with her.

I don't know how long I was in that place with the angels before I began to hear someone calling my name. I was being summoned back to my body from the realm of the angels. When I had fully "come back" and was clearly in the present, I discovered that I had been journeying for almost two hours. It seemed like a short journey to the different levels of consciousness while I was in it! Along with the beautiful experience of the angel meditation, I also learned that the passage of time is very different in the other realm!

***

Angels are very good at providing confirmation to us of their presence and of their handiwork. After my experience with the angels in the guided meditation, I received the validation and confirmation that what I had witnessed was real, and that there were other people that had seen similar forms of angels. I was really starting to trust that validation of my personal experiences with angels, spirit guides and spirit overall would come to me; I didn't have to search for it. One month later, I received a happy validation of my vision of the thousands of tiny angels streaming from the larger angel's blue cape.

I was visiting an old friend in another city, and this friend's son had just come through a bone marrow transplant for leukemia. It was a very scary time for her, watching as her son fought fevers and infection after the transplant.

When his fevers finally ended and he was feeling better, she asked him, "Weren't you scared? You were really sick for a long time."

He replied, "No, I wasn't scared at all. The angels stayed with me every day."

He described how the angels drew pictures high up on the wall of his hospital room and tried to make him laugh. He told her they were very, very small angels and they were always near the ceiling.

"One day," he said, "they told me that I would be fine and then they all left."

His mom asked him if he had seen them again since that day and he told her no.

"I didn't need their help any more so they left", he said. He never questioned whether what he saw was real because he knew they were real.

When I heard his description of the tiny angels, I knew he had seen the angels as I had seen them in my guided angel meditation, and it was confirmation and validation for me. I had never before seen an angel that small, nor had I any knowledge they even existed in that form. But it is clear that I could learn much more about them if I hung out in the children's hospital. Kids see lots of things and instinctively know much more about angels, fairies and other cosmic helpers than a lot of adults do!

Getting confirmation that you have experienced the intervention or presence of an angel is as simple as asking for it. You can even ask for three confirmations, which a lot of people do. If you trust that you really are receiving confirmation or validation then you probably only need to receive it once, but for skeptics and people less confident, three confirmations seems to be enough to make them accept their life has been graced by angels.

CHAPTER 6

Meditations with Spirit

On a typical day I will "sit with Spirit" for about an hour in the morning. Sitting with Spirit is my time to sit in silence, meditate, send healing out, and/or work on blending with Spirit to strengthen my link with these energies. I close my sit-time with my usual question, "I am going to end this session now, is there anything you want me to know before I stop?" Sometimes I will see a clairvoyant image or instantly "know" information. I used to sit only one or two days a week but I really strengthened my link to Spirit when I began sitting every day. This also provided me with a time to work on my own spiritual and personal healing, as well as sending out healing.

Any person wishing to develop their mediumship must recognize that personal healing and self-awareness is part of your development and growth as a healer (and as a person). Mediumship is healing in all its forms. The path of a medium is an ongoing personal growth workshop. "Healer, heal thyself" and "know thyself" do have relevance! One benefit I found very early on in this daily practice was that my clairaudience began to increase. I had never put focused effort to strengthening it; I just accepted it as part of the overall intuitive package that is me.

Meditation was pretty hard for me in the beginning. I used to think it was either useless or meant for people who were more spiritually evolved than me. My first few weeks attempting to meditate usually ended because I fell asleep. I never imagined I would one day be able to sit in meditation for over an hour.

Meditation can mean many different things. To some, meditation is sitting and musing—thinking casually about stuff. To others, meditation means completely stilling the mind of any chatter or noise. To me, meditation is my *meditative time*. How I use that meditative time can vary from quieting my thoughts to beaming healing energy to the world. Regardless of how I have chosen to spend my meditative time, it always involves quieting my mind and creating some space between thoughts. Ideally, to be able to sit and take a mental step back and rest my strong mind by shelving it for a while—to not think—is only one way that I meditate. Sending out healing vibes, or smiling with your liver (just as some traditional Balinese medicine men advise), still requires a level of thought and intent, even if minimal.

Included in my meditative time is my "sit" time. I spend sitting time in meditative thought and process, quieting my mind first before I start any process. I concentrate on:

+ Balancing my own energies

+ Blending with my spirit team

+ Connecting with Spirit, my higher self and the great healing mind/spirit/source

It is my quiet time bonding with all that is God. It is also the space from which I send healing to others, and send my thanks and gratitude to angels, guides, spirit people, ascended masters, and so on. It is the time and space where my guides, angels and spirit helpers give me information and guidance. My meditations are heart opening, chakra clearing, grounding and centering, prayerful, peaceful, restful, inspiring and healing. I have received premonitions, predictions, warnings, guidance, reassurance, inspiration and healing. I've become one with the universe and filled up with stars, transported through walls and experienced time standing still. All this and more from making the commitment to show up for my regular meditation!

If you are strong-minded like me, you will discover that a regular meditation time will help your mind get used to giving up control. When you are working with Spirit or your psychic skills, that strong mind must take a back seat so your guides and other energies on the psychic airwaves can get through to you.

***

Have you ever told yourself, "I've been meditating for weeks and nothing has happened. I suck at this." You worry about it and build up negative energy. This energy floats around, growing bigger, and you become convinced that you will forever suck at meditation.

This is what my angel Josephine meant when she said, "I want you to see the grey". She showed me a vision that I could easily understand – sludgy grey slushy snow. This snow had been driven over and over by cars and was now a grey sludge that was building with each passing car. This grey sludge was thoughts, our **negative** thoughts. She showed me how our negative thoughts float away from us and begin to build. When these negative thoughts (or sludge) reach a certain level, they begin to create more sludge **on their own**. It begins to feed itself! All our thoughts, which **are** energy, are out in our world and constantly around us. If we continually have, create or emit negative thoughts, we are responsible for giving "the grey" the power to grow. Until I understood this, I was an oblivious contributor to the creation of "the grey".

All those sayings about thinking positive and changing our negative mindsets really are important to keep in mind and practice. Do you want to be responsible for creating grey sludge? I don't. I am not willing to be responsible for the creation of negativity and sludge in my universe. Emotional distress, angry outbursts, bad moods, blocked chakras and so on can be attributed to the accumulation of grey sludge. Grey sludge-like thoughts that just keep piling up can create an energy mass that is out of control.

Your thoughts are filled with your energy. Someone once said, "Please take responsibility for the energy you bring into this space". If you are stuck in days of negative thinking, do your best to find a way back to a clear energy level.

Years ago I attended a conference where Neale Donald Walsh, author of the book *Conversations With God*, was speaking. He spoke of just these types of days and he provided this tip that I still think about whenever I find myself slipping on sludge. The tip is, "Find your ticket back in to the flow". Your ticket could a hug, a pampering long bath, a walk by the water or in the forest or some meditative time. It could be watching a movie that makes you laugh until your cheeks hurt. Find your ticket and then remember it for those days when your thoughts are grey. And make a **conscious** choice to shift your thoughts to the positive energy. It may feel very hard to do in the moment, but you **can** do it and, you'll be "back in the flow" pretty quickly.

CHAPTER 7

Testing the Contract

A number of years after having no night-time visitors and with my children out of their teen years, I thought that it would be alright to loosen the boundaries of my "contract" and allow Spirit to connect with me during the night time if there was an emergency. I was thinking this would be if an emergency arose with my family members and such. At this point in my life I was divorced, and I was in a relationship with a new partner. We lived together in a house thousands of miles away from my children who were now adults living in their own homes.

The very same day I told Spirit that it was okay to reach out for an emergency, I was awakened in the middle of the night. I was awakened with the feeling that someone was trying to get my attention. When I opened my eyes, I saw a large glowing white orb up in one corner of the bedroom ceiling. I blinked hard, thinking I must be seeing things through sleepy eyes but the white orb was still there, looking like a ball of mist slowly circling.

I closed my eyes and without moving I said to my boyfriend (just loud enough to wake him up), "Will you please look at the ceiling and tell me if you see anything?"

I asked him to do this so I could ensure that I really was seeing the orb. He said he could see a white ball of mist near the ceiling. Ok, so I wasn't crazy.

It was not difficult to tune in to the spirit energy that was requesting my attention and when I did, I received details about who she was and what her emergency was. The lady in spirit that was reaching out was a stranger to me but I was the medium she was connecting with, so of course I would help if I could. She conveyed to me that her death was as a result of a car accident on a stretch of road that was dark with almost no traffic. She was caught by surprise as her car ran off the road, flipping and causing her death. New to the spirit world, she was not sure what to do—so she reached out and managed to connect with me. Maybe it was because I had just that day agreed to take the night shift for emergencies. I did the only thing I knew to do: I asked for Spirit and angels to assist this lovely spirit in her new journey. I sent her love and then waited for her, and the orb that was her energy, to move along with the help of her spirit family.

As I kept my eyes closed during the link with Spirit, I asked my boyfriend to tell me if he saw any change in the orb. He told me that the orb slowly moved along the ceiling and then disappeared through the wall to the outside. I knew she had successfully moved along and was safely united with her spirit family. Once this was done, the energy in the bedroom and the persistent sense of someone wanting my attention dissipated. And then I reinstated my contract to once again include no waking me up at night.

I have tested the contract at different times and Spirit has honored it on all occasions. Sometimes things we ask for are slow to manifest and other times the response is instant. I learned many things from this little "test", and certainly I learned to be very clear and specific about what I ask for. I also gained an even deeper awareness of how responsive Spirit can be. There may never be a shortage of persons in spirit wishing to communicate with us, and for some people the door is always open for contact at any time. I know I function much better on a good night's sleep and I think Spirit knows that too.

To develop a respectful working relationship with the spirit world was something I never knew was possible or was even necessary. I no longer worry about missing an emergency call from family, for they really were the people that I was most worried about—my kids, my family and friends. I have had more experiences where Spirit has shown me they can reach out to me any time and any place if necessary and appropriate. To this day, I am still grateful for that initial piece of advice to set up a contract with Spirit. It made me look honestly at what I was willing to do in service to Spirit. I believe that is why my contract is unchanged after all these years, with the exception of that one night hiccup.

CHAPTER 8

Personal Growth Continues

You hear over and over again that Spirit is always near, and always sending you love. During my years of client sessions and meditation, I scribbled many enlightening notes and messages on scraps of paper. For a long time they just piled up; I never really reviewed all my scribbles so I never really grasped the consistency of the messages. Two statements are always there: "We are here" and "We will never leave you." I used to think that other mediums were just stating the "nice to have" wishes that we want our benevolent beings in spirit to have for us. But they aren't just niceties said for convenience or for compliment. Spirit has shown this to me in my personal life and in the lives of my clients. They are there for us.

My father passed away in 1999. He had no religious beliefs and if he did end up in a church it was because he had to be there, at the request of someone else or to fulfill a duty. His motto truly was "everything is mind over matter". He went to weddings and funerals but other than that he had no interest. He never expressed any spiritual interest and certainly did not go for discussions about enlightenment, life after death or angels. So when he passed away I naturally assumed that I would never hear from him in the spirit world. I thought that his spirit would just move along and do whatever he wanted—which surely would not include making his presence known on this side of the veil.

For a number of years there was no sign of him. Other mediums that tried to contact him (for their own curiosity or practice) were not successful. It was what it was and it never bothered me since I accepted that he would have had no interest.

About five or six years after his death, on an ordinary day I suddenly became aware of the smell of pipe tobacco. No one smoked a pipe in my house and he was the only person I thought of whenever I did smell that particular scent so I thought, "Oh, could that be Dad?" Then, in my mind was pressed a word, almost like a blunt statement, "Bruce." Bruce is my brother. What also came with the name was a sense of something pending. What I later understood was this name-dropping was his way of saying, "Something's up with your brother, pay attention." Staying true to his minimal communicative style, he never did anything else.

My Dad's visits were rare; on very occasional days he would bring his energy in, state the name of one of my siblings, and then withdraw his energy. He never made his presence known in any other way until just a few years ago.

That year, I was taking part in a development workshop when he suddenly came through another medium with a message for me. Now, my father was not particularly emotive, never said "I love you", and hugs were like saluting—only when absolutely necessary. So a message from my dad that said, "I'm sorry I wasn't there for you before. I'm here now." was really hard for me to accept. It seemed out of character for him. But I was grateful for the message even if I couldn't quite believe it was really him.

Over the next two days of the workshop, I received the same message from four different mediums. Now I know that when we travel to the spirit realm we have a grander world and cosmic understanding; we view and remember who we are at the soul level. Knowing that all souls can remember and hence find enlightenment, or be re-enlightened, still did not convince me that he was really saying those words.

However, three months after the workshop, he did something incredible that gave me a new insight about how even the most non-spiritual, non-believing people can be greatly surprised once they cross over into the realm of spirit. I'm sure you have heard many times how we will remember who we are, what we are and we will re-remember how the universe works overall once we cross to the spirit realm. It is one thing to grasp this concept and believe it. It is quite another thing and, incredibly exciting and affirming, to hear it directly from someone you know in spirit.

A few months after that workshop, during one of my typical morning meditations, I asked my closing question as usual, "I am going to end this session now, is there anything you want me to know before I stop?"

This day, right after I asked Spirit my closing question, I heard very loudly, clearly, and directly beside my right ear "I **am** alive!"

It was my father's voice. I cannot express how shocked I was to hear his voice filled with an excitement I have **never** heard in him. Plus, I also heard the familiar determination in his voice that he often had when trying to impress a point or enforce a rule. I heard his shock and excitement and his determined voice making sure I got the message! Well, I got it loud and clear! After more than ten years of none-to-minimal communication from him except for the curt name-dropping, he did this. And, he made it very clear he was just as shocked as I was to know that he suddenly realized that he really was still alive. I'm not sure who was more surprised, him or me, although from how it sounded, I think it was him. The best part was to hear the excitement in his voice and to hear him deliver his message with the sternness for which he was known. But I also had to ask, "Why did it take him so long?"

Time is not the same in the spirit world as it is here so I can understand at that level but, why did it take **him** so long to discover his new existence? I know that sometimes a spirit needs time to practice and perfect the art of communicating with us in our dense physical realm, but I never thought it could take ten years. Whether it was his own frame of mind as a non-believer or whether he needed healing or just a long time to adjust to his new reality, I don't know yet. Perhaps one day he will be able to tell me more about his life in the spirit world. For now, I think he has figured out how that mind-over-matter stuff works.

***

There are different reasons why it can take longer than we expect for a spirit to communicate with us. A few weeks after my own father's visit, I met a young woman whose father had passed ten years ago. Despite her hopeful visits to mediums and psychics, he had not made his presence known to them, nor to her.

On this particular day I was having a casual Sunday brunch with my friend and her guest Emily, who was quite pregnant. I had just finished an evening of spirit communication the night before and now it was my day off. I wasn't "working"; I was having a nice meal. While we waited for our plates of food to arrive, Emily started telling me that no-one had been able to bring her father through (he had died ten years prior). She thought it was because she had been very angry with him for dying. I suggested that it was Ok if she was angry with him for dying but perhaps she really had **not** wanted to hear from him.

I asked, "Are you ready to hear from him now?"

She thought about this for a moment, laughed, and in a voice full of emotion said, "Yes, I think I am ready. But maybe that's just the baby hormones talking."

She patted her growing baby belly. And then our plates of food arrived. I think I got through half my eggs when I suddenly felt the very strong presence of a spirit person standing beside me. He was tall and had a white coat on, like a lab coat. Her father had arrived. Surprise!

When I am enjoying a meal with friends, I try very hard to stick to my own rules and not speak about spirit presence unless it is appropriate. I never want to invade or force. Sometimes though, I have no choice but to honor the wishes of the spirit communicator and open up the conversation. This girl's father was pressing so hard on me, almost like he decided to sit down **on** me that I really had to say something.

"Um, I need to let you know something and I hope it is okay to tell you this but I believe your father has just arrived."

"Really? How do you know and why would he suddenly show up after all these years?" she asked.

I would have asked the same thing—in fact I did just that when my own father appeared after ten or so years.

I began to describe to her the man I could see clairvoyantly, and provided details that confirmed to her that it really was her father in spirit. He not only confirmed his job but also said some very particular and personal messages that only she knew. So there we were sitting in the restaurant; she was in tears, but filled with joy and shock. Her father came straight away to her once she decided that she was ready to hear from him. Once she let go of her anger toward him for dying (and he spoke to that issue in his dialogue through me), he came. I was filled with the incredible love he had for her, his daughter.

This father's visit, so closely following my own father's visit and announcement, reinforced for me the knowledge that sometimes spirit people are learning how to communicate with us and it can take a long time. But since time is not the same in the spirit world as it is for us, we may find that to be years. It also taught me that sometimes, some people need to reach a point where they can let go of their anger or whatever holds them back from accepting communication from their loved ones in spirit. It's not a fault, no one is to blame. Spirit will respect our state—just as they respectfully stood in my bedroom doorway waiting for me—and when we are ready, or need them, they will be there.

Spirit is here for us, they will never leave us because they never have. Only the physical form has left us or 'been discarded'. Their soul, spirit, essence, energy, mind—whatever you want to name it, lives forever and has moved into a different form, the *next* way of being.

When I was writing this section about Emily and her father, I checked in with her for permission to include it and she shared with me how she still remembers our day at the restaurant a few years ago. In her words: *"I have thought about that lunch almost daily since it happened. It has given me so much peace."* And Emily's peace and healing also heals and brings peace to her father. We can heal and build bridges to and for each other, on both sides of the veil.

CHAPTER 9

Lighting the Night

I have met many "night lightworkers". These are individuals that fulfill their lightworker roles in the astral plane while they sleep. Some people really like the feeling of waking up with memories of a lucid dream. Most intuitively know they are helping on another plane but want to find a way to bring that ability into their waking hours. For some others, "night work" is a safe way to utilize their psychic abilities and not have to face them in the bright of day. It can be comfortable to do your work only in dream state. If you have a profound experience, you might write it in your journal and think no more of it. Or you might be shaken or disturbed by a trip to the astral plane and then dread sleep, causing you insomnia.

Some feel they have no control in their dreams; but you **can** have control in your night work, in your dreams.

The astral plane is a wonderful way for your angels, spirit guides and loved ones to capture your complete attention! I have often heard people say that they keep getting messages and speaking to people in their dreams, but they either can't figure out what to do with the information or experience, or they don't know why it is happening to them.

I have met people that help souls cross over to the light, have comforted and kept company to souls while their physical body is dying, and have given information and received messages for others, all in the dream or astral plane. I have met people that have travelled around the globe, and have had endless discussions with both loved ones in spirit, angels, spirit guides and animals. Sometimes these astral travellers and dreamers are at the scene of a tragedy—either before or after the event. Sometimes they visit their own future, or a past life or many lives. No matter what is happening, lightwork is happening, healing is happening It's either happening **to** you, or you are helping where you are needed. One person I know has been a night worker all her life. She has been blessed to be aware of her astral travel, and has helped many souls in transition. It doesn't have to be a traumatic, scary, frightening or frustrating experience for you. You are doing night work for a reason. At some point in the journey of your soul, you **agreed** to do it!

Most likely your daily living experience is filled with events or experiences that have made it near impossible for the spirit world and psychic information to reach your mind. Sometimes it is fear of seeing something unpleasant, of being frightened of what we don't know or understand, that causes the spirit realm to utilize our time of sleep as the time to reach out. A person heavily grieving the loss of a loved one may only find solace in dreams, when the mind is at rest, letting the other "airwaves" of communication open up.

The most frustrated individuals I meet are trying to shift their dream work to the daytime. For most people, it not so much making a shift away from something, but making an addition *to* your daytime awareness. You will always have the natural ability to visit the astral plane while sleeping. The content of your dream experiences may change when you begin to work with Spirit during the daytime; this is what night workers notice and dislike the most. Similar to leaving one job behind that you knew inside-out and beginning another one, it is going to feel and be different from what you have experienced and are comfortable with. If you can accept and know that you will not be losing anything, only shifting awareness, then you are placing your mindset at optimal openness to experience a new way of communicating and working with the spirit world, all other energies and your psychic senses. Also, it may very well be that the spirit world wants and is nudging you towards shifting the bulk of your focus to the daytime hours.

Why would Spirit want you to make this shift? Perhaps to start helping all the people you come in contact with every day. The spirit world wants to let us know they are still alive and communicating; if you shift you focus towards lightwork during the daytime, it creates the opportunity for you to reach out and touch one of Spirit's relatives here and now. Perhaps your angels have something specific in mind that they need your help with on a Monday at 2:00 p.m. You will be instrumental in bringing healing and joy to both the spirit world **and** the living. That is worth a shift in awareness!

How you begin to shift and grow your awareness begins with you accepting that you are the focus of a cosmic nudge and you are a part of the whole grand workings of the galaxy we live in, and of the expanding universe we also live in. The spark of divine light, the force majeure is within you still. You are linked with everything there is, so of course you can speak to Spirit in the astral plane, just as you can receive divine guidance during meditation or feel an angel's embrace in a dark moment. You may not feel like a healer or lightworker, but since that divine spark **is** healing and love, that ability is already within your soul. You are already a spirit having the human experience right now. So since you are already a spirit, and have a human body, why not let that spirit work through the human?

CHAPTER 10

Oh, That Was Unexpected

My work has always brought me surprising and unexpected events and connections. Some make a big impact while others provide quiet insights and glimpses of the great network behind the scenes; here are a few of those experiences.

Memories of a Past Life

I have learned that anything is possible when working with Spirit. I just have to relay the information that comes through, without analyzing it. Sometimes the information reveals how a past life can influence a current life.

Jenn had a clear connection to earth and animal energies; she had an incredibly deep bond with animals. She asked for a reading to help her learn more about this connection. During her reading it became clear that Jenn was very worried and upset about the health of her horse, a beautiful 14-year-old Arabian. The animal was in constant pain with a lame hip and knee and Jenn had run out of ideas for treatment. There was no apparent reason for the horse's pain: no injury present, no infection, just pain.

As Jenn explained how guilty she felt about the horse's pain, I began to sense a spirit presence coming up behind me. Suddenly I felt a strong but gentle nudge in my back—from a horse! I had never before felt the warmth and strength of a spirit horse standing directly behind me.

My eyes must have widened as I said, "Ummm, I have a....horse here. She tells me she belongs to you."

As I described the spirit horse, Jenn confirmed that this was indeed her horse—a mare that had passed away several years ago. As I linked with the mare's spirit, I could feel a deep love and gratitude for her life with Jenn. But then I started receiving vivid clairvoyant images of Jenn and her current horse, the Arabian, in another time and location as a past life.

The flashing images showed Jenn as a man, dressed in long dark robes, riding an Arabian horse in a battle. The horse was struck in the knee by a spiked metal ball, in the hip by a sword. Then the next "snapshot" showed the man (Jenn) lying with the injured horse, cradling its head as the animal died. This man felt tremendous grief and responsibility for the death of his horse.

As I relayed the information and detail of these images to Jenn, tears welled up in her eyes and she began to shake.

She said, "I've always felt instinctively that I rode my horse into battle. I think that is why I feel so responsible for every pain that my horse feels in this lifetime."

This was my first experience with a spirit horse in a session. I had no knowledge of what a horse might be thinking, remembering or wanting to say but it was very clear that this spirit animal was able to provide information to me. The information and messages for Jenn from her beloved spirit horse and from her loved ones in spirit provided me with the words to say, and I just let them flow out of me as quickly as I received them. Spirit reminded her that in that previous lifetime she was expected to ride her own horse into battle. The enemy's weapons had killed the horse, not her, and she was no longer required to carry guilt for that. Spirit went on to say that in her life now, she is a loving, responsible and compassionate caregiver to her horses. I could see the relief and weight of guilt and responsibility lift off her chest and shoulders as I passed even more information to her about her lifetime with this horse. Spirit let me know that she and the Arabian had a soulmate bond.

Before the session ended, one of my spirit healers suggested using a specific type of birch paste, and some other substances, on the horse's painful hip and knee. I asked her if she knew what the spirit healer meant.

Her eyes few open and she said, "Yes, I've heard of this paste but I've never used it."

The spirit healer then provided some instructions for further energy healing techniques to assist with the healing of the horse.

***

I always learn something from Spirit. Each contact, whether person or animal, is new and brings evidence of loving support from the other side. Just as we humans want to let our animal friends know we love them, our beloved pets of all kinds in spirit want to let us know they love us still.

Mary of Bethany

I was staying at a bed and breakfast facility in Vancouver before moving to a new apartment. One morning I woke up at 5:30 a.m. and decided to read because the room, so lovely and quiet, was being lit by the rising sun. The floor I was staying on had six separate bedrooms and everyone else was asleep. There were no traffic noises and I felt like I had the entire world to myself. I dove into my book.

Suddenly I felt a wave of pressure streaming down into the room! I looked up and saw a figure standing at the end of my bed. The figure was not solid but was very clearly a woman dressed in long robes with a hood. She appeared to be very tall, probably a lot taller than when she was alive, but this tall-effect I knew to be the visual effect of the streaming energy. I was surprised at the visit and also at her very strong presence!

Then she said, "I am Mary of Bethany".

I was not familiar with biblical names or references so I thought, "Who the heck is that?" but I actually said, "Umm...who?"

She repeated her name.

I said, "Welcome. Thank you for coming. Do you have a message for me?" (Whether the message is conveyed telepathically or through my clairaudience it doesn't matter. Spirit always gets the message across.)

This message was for a resident guest on my floor. Mary of Bethany wanted me to tell him, "Expect a miracle. There will be a healing in three months." She wanted me to deliver it to him right away and with those exact words.

Now that's a big, impactful message and although awesome, I had to make sure it really was meant for the person she intended.

So I said, "Ok, if this is really for him, and you want it delivered right away, you are going to have to find a way to put him at my door because he's asleep and I don't want to wake him up—he might think I'm nuts".

And then Mary of Bethany was gone as swiftly as she had appeared, taking with her all the feelings of pressure and energy. It's a strange feeling when a spirit visitor suddenly leaves after bringing such powerful and loving energy into my space. I felt like I had exhaled and in between breaths there was a silent void.

I strolled over to my door and opened it, just in case my housemate (and soon to be recipient of the message) appeared. I sat down on my bed to wait, and then I heard a door open. He walked right by my open door. Ok, I thought to myself, I **am** to deliver this message to him! I was excited and worried at the same time; he had no idea that I was a medium or clairvoyant. We didn't really know much about each other. What if he didn't want the message? What if it freaked him out?

I walked over to him as he was heading across the floor to the kitchen. I first asked him if he was religious. He said no, but he was raised Catholic and considered himself to be spiritual more than religious. I felt relieved and began to tell him that I had received a visitor from Spirit with a message for him. Had he ever heard of Mary of Bethany?

My guest house roommate, who I will call "Pete" here, was married with a young child. Pete's wife had suffered a traumatic injury and was at a rehabilitation facility nearby. Caring for his wife and son meant losing income and the family home. All three were living apart until affordable and accessible housing could be found. It was a huge and traumatic shift of life for this family.

So I delivered the message and told him about Mary of Bethany, the visitor from Spirit. He was clearly moved and tears came to his eyes. He asked if this meant his wife would recover to full health again, but I did not have that answer. All I could say was that miracles and healings come in many different ways—sometimes not the way we think it will appear. Our job is to trust and let God and Spirit take care of the details.

I don't know if Pete's wish for his wife to be restored to full health was fulfilled; the last time I spoke with him, her strength had greatly improved and there was still hope. I do know that three months after I relayed the message from Spirit, the family received housing and funding so they could all be together again under one roof. Their greatest fear—not knowing if they had a future together—may have been relieved by Mary of Bethany.

I did some research after this visit from Spirit; I often do this when I am contacted by a spirit that appears to be wearing significantly different clothing or provides a well-known historical name. I do this research because I usually have no idea who these people were when they were alive. Doing this kind of research has helped me identify and find more information, which is always fascinating. It seems that Mary of Bethany was from Bethany, a village near Jerusalem. In the Bible story, she was the person who washed Jesus' feet with perfume. She was also the sister of Lazarus and Martha. After Jesus' death she created a healing community and cared for the infirm. When I read about her healing work I then understood why she had come to bring the message of healing.

Star People

One day I was at the end of my meditative time with Spirit and, as usual, I asked if there is anything they wanted me to know. I heard, "One hundred to three hundred star-people are being released to the planet to assist with a critical traumatic event." Then a vision followed.

It appeared to be night time and the landscape was very rocky. A silver object was lying far down at the bottom of some place/thing. Nearby to the silver object I saw star- people arriving—each one appearing in a flash, like bright blinks of white light. They arrived one by one at an incredible speed, all together in the same place. They were ready to accompany every soul crossing over during this event.

The star-people impressed upon me how concerned they were about the care of our souls. They described the huge team that works for us, and we are totally unaware of them. But they care greatly about us and have concern for each and every one of our souls.

The speed at which each star-person arrived in the flashes of light was faster than I can even describe. They were arriving before the event happened, and it was clear that they were all going to be in place and ready.

As a follow-up to this vision, three days later on a commercial airliner crashed in the Alps and all 150 on board were killed. When I heard of this event, and saw the location of the crash, I knew immediately that this was the traumatic event that the star-people had described. I also knew that each person on the flight, each soul crossing over, was instantaneously met by a star-person and escorted safely to their next destination.

Some time later I happened to be working at a church fundraiser and met a gentleman who was much more knowledgeable about the world of spirit than I, with decades of experience under his belt. He happened to say the word "star-people" in the course of our conversation and of course my ears perked up for I had never heard anyone else use that word in relation to the spirit world. This man gave me his explanation of what he thought star-people were. He believed them to be highly evolved spirit beings that perform a very high level of important work with relation to the care and well-being of our souls. Considering that I had not told this gentleman of my experience and message from the star-people, I was very happy for his validation of their important role, as they had shown me.

Some will wonder why the spirit helpers called themselves "star-people". As I do with all my private sittings and meditations, I relay the words and the sentences, just as I receive them. Perhaps my mind understands "star-people" better than other words. Perhaps the words *are* right, considering we are all made of star-stuff. What I do know is that we have help in forms we may not be completely aware of or be able to pin a title to.

Around the world there are plane crashes, natural disasters, wars and accidents that claim the lives of many every day. The vision and message provided to me from the star-people may have been regarding only one critical event but the knowledge they gave me let me know that no matter how many incidents are taking place around the globe, their response is the same. Ready before and at the moment they are needed to be there for us at our time of transition. As horrible as the actual event was, and as events can be, I know now that there is much more care for our soul's well-being than I had ever imagined.

CHAPTER 11

What I See When I'm Working

When beginning a session with a client, I always bless our space, perform a grounding ceremony for my sitter, and myself, and set the intention that I am open to receive. For me, this means that my entire "antenna", my full body, mind and heart are open and waiting for input. I am relaxed and trust that what is meant to arrive will arrive. I am aware of any sensations: telepathic, emotional and physical. There are mediums that experience noises in the room with the presence of spirit people (as I do sometimes as well), such as cracking or knocking sounds in the walls.

Angels, guides and spirit helpers all arrive on different vibrations and frequencies but they all know my working frequency. So they tune down towards my frequency and I tune up towards theirs in order for us to communicate. I get holographic images and impressions from all of them: visual impressions of scenes or persons, emotions, messages and personality.

This is especially true for me with information from the spirit world. The information can be so detailed that it is like downloading an entire e-book into my brain and senses all at once. Those who have worked with me know this is why I might say in a session, "I'm just going to be quiet for a moment and listen to, or watch, what Spirit is giving me".

***

I have always seen spirit people clairvoyantly in black and white, but with touches of color—that is, the clothing and hair appeared with color. When the young man in spirit wearing the colorful patchwork shirt stood in my doorway; I immediately saw the shirt. When I saw that same shirt on a living person I realized that the colorful shirt on the spirit person was **meant** to grab my attention so that I could spot that spirit's friend walking up the driveway next door.

I have seen a gentleman in spirit (who died in a car crash) wearing a blue shirt with blood on the chest area. That vision was not gross, or bloody; it was just like looking at a blue shirt with red on it. The impressions he sent me told me about his accident. He included an image of the steering wheel impacting him on the chest, and at the same time I felt heavy pressure on **my** chest.

The night my boyfriend died in a motorcycle accident, he showed me an image of him lying on the road in a pool of blood; it was not frightening. It just was a scene containing a whole lot of information and images, although charged with emotion.

For me, spirit people (deceased loved ones) have no temperature with their presence except that on occasion, I may feel a slight drop in temperature either close by me or in the room. If this happens to you, **don't worry**! It is not a sign something bad is happening; there is no need to think it's a creepy spirit. If it makes you feel uncomfortable, simply say hello to acknowledge that you are aware of your spirit visitor. Then ask the visitor to warm the space back up. It is important to acknowledge that presence because your loved one in spirit is working hard to reach you.

Sometimes I feel a sensation of pressure quickly build in the room and sometimes I feel the energy of that spirit very close beside me. Often it feels like the energy is pushing on, through or on top of me. Sometimes, depending on the spirit's ability, I will be able to externally see (objectively) their energy in the space as the spirit passes in front of me or enters the room. This sensation or sight is not troubling. In fact, now that I know what it is, I admire those in spirit for their efforts to be present.

The very first time I saw spirit energy in a session I was immediately struck by just how much effort and energy is needed for spirit to appear at all. I gained a much clearer understanding of why a spirit would find the most efficient shape, form and manner to connect with us. I understood then that when I did see this effort by a spirit, it was someone trying hard to get a message through to this side.

Hearing a spirit person speak to me, both objectively and subjectively, has taken me a number of years to develop and I will always continue to develop it further. I may also receive smells, such as grandfather's pipe tobacco or mom's perfume, with my "inner" nose psychic sense called clairgustance.

***

Angels are a little different from spirit visitors; they each have a unique color, light and frequency. Angels communicate to me in much the same way as I receive all my information (hearing, images, words, knowledge, etc.) but they bring the distinctive energy of a higher evolution and higher purpose. Whether it is the chills that Archangel Michael flushes through my entire physical body or the hot heat that Archangel Chamuel brings to my head and chest, archangels and angels **feel** different to me from deceased loved ones.

I gave a workshop shortly after I began to work with the angelic realm. While I was teaching, I noticed (clairvoyance) a stream of light begin to descend from the ceiling off to my left side. As the stream of light began to take on a purple color, it also increased in height and width. My ears began to ring a very high ringing buzz and I felt a strong wave of pressure build with the purple stream's growth.

I stopped talking and asked, "Who has just arrived?"

Immediately I heard and felt (clairaudience and clairsentience) the giant Archangel Metatron. From ceiling to floor, 20 feet from top to bottom, the wide purple light flowed. It was clearly a living light with a vibration, intelligence and lots of beautiful color. The workshop participants also felt the shift in the room, with most feeling a sudden rush of heat and pressure. Of course I used this opportunity to have the participants tune in to the energy; they knew something big was happening in our space. So we welcomed the great Archangel Metatron to our workshop and thanked him for being with us.

Archangel Metatron visited our workshop the next day, too. We were very blessed to have this experience, and from that day forward I perceived Archangels this way—as streams of light, color and vibration. They then link with my thoughts and provide any information they wish to impart. Angels, different from Archangels, also "feel" different to me but again, I am instantly aware of their highly evolved consciousness, high vibration and protection. There is more to the angelic realm than angels and archangels, and completely worth your time and effort to discover.

***

A **spirit guide** always opens communication with me by announcing that he or she is a guide. It is always clear that spirit guides take their roles seriously; they are strongly dedicated to their task of being your guides. In my years of working with people and also with my own guides, I have found that each person has at least one dedicated spirit guide who stays with that person for the entire lifetime. Other spirit guides may work with us for a period of time and then switch out with another guide as needed. This is all dependent on what you are doing with your life, what you are learning (or needing to learn), and also to keep you on the track or path of the current life that your soul has come to experience. **You** are their highest priority. It's the job of your entire team—your spirit guides, angels and spirit helpers—to look after your soul and its journey while living in this human form. Every person has their own crew of "roadies" working behind the scenes and sometimes out in front, to make sure your soul receives what it is meant to experience. And then, your crew of roadies will ensure your soul makes the journey "home" safely. And they do it because they want to; you are cherished.

***

Orbs are an efficient and effective form for spirit consciousness. The sphere has been suggested as the most efficient shape because it takes less energy for a spirit to create an orb. Some people see angels in the form of orbs (or consider orbs to be angels). An orb can contain just one consciousness or it can contain many. I can feel orbs when they are close to my body and in a room. They too feel like a pressure on my body and aura.

I was so curious about the energies I felt during my meditative time that I set up my camera to video myself sitting in meditation. During that first video, I made mental notes of where I felt energy moving around or on me, and also whom I sensed was with me. Then I watched the video and saw orbs of different sizes moving through the room and over me. I was able to watch my two guides for the first time ever as they moved around me, stopped at my hands, my heart, one side of my head and then the other.

I also sometimes see orbs with my physical eyes, during sessions with some clients or other times when Spirit wants my attention. Orbs on film can be any color. For me, the orbs I physically see in daylight appear white and rather transparent. Spirit visitors, spirit guides and angels have also appeared to me as very bright flashes of light. Sometimes this flash is white, sometimes another color. Sometimes, there are a few winking and flashing in the room. I have learned that for me, this is their signal that they want me to know they are there and also to let my client know they are there for them as well. Many of my clients have stated that they too had seen the flashes but did not know if it was just their eyes playing tricks or if it was something electrical turning on and off.

I get so much joy from working with spirit and from having their presence in my daily life. It is so fun to know that my spirit helpers get just as excited as I do when something very special is in the works. A few years ago I had a trip planned to England to do some intensive mediumship study at the prestigious Arthur Findlay College for Psychic Studies and for three weeks prior to the course I had more orbs and bright lights blinking around my home than I could count! Spirit was very excited that I was going to be attending the College and they certainly let me know. It was pretty fun because it was like having a bunch of excited bubbles around and underfoot, which really made me chuckle.

***

These are my personal styles of receiving and sensing. You may experience some similar things. Your experiences may be totally different from mine. It does not matter if you sense 1 way or 10 ways, it is knowing your personal ways of sensing and receiving information psychically—intuitively that is important. And our intuitive senses can grow and strengthen. For some, this happens all on its own without any direction or training. Typically most people find that a structure like a workshop or course of study helps focus fine tune skills. I have benefitted greatly from the workshops and study I have completed. Exposure to different and new exercises from a variety of sources and teachers lets us learn and try out things. All this provides us with new experiences and knowledge. It also helps us find our own truths and certainties.

CHAPTER 12

Maybe Your Child Sees...

How can parents tell if their child is truly seeing spirit people or angels as opposed to having a vivid imagination or a bad dream? When a parent asks this question it tells me that the parent is, even in some small way, open to all possibilities. Psychic, mediumistic, intuitive, empathic or "clair" experiences can happen to anyone, but when your child says there are people waking him/her up at night and the child is afraid to sleep in his/her own bedroom, it is distressing to both child and parent. Our "clair" senses can be overwhelming at any age if you do not know how those senses perceive energetic and invisible energies and then deliver that received information to your nervous system. A young child unable to understand or describe sensations or communicate feelings in words could be expressing them as bad dreams, avoidance, tantrum, or fears including fear of the dark.

Many have discovered that very young children — toddlers — are quite comfortable remembering former lives and talking about their "imaginary" friends. This seems to change as the child gets older. Each child will differ in how he or she perceives, reacts and shares psychic experiences. One eight-year-old child suddenly developed a great reluctance to go to bed and then began to wake in the middle of the night crying and frightened because people were waking her up and talking to her. She refused to go back to bed, and only agreed to go if a parent stayed with her until she fell asleep. After a few months of disrupted sleep for everyone, the parents contacted me to see if I could discover what might be going on.

This mother was open-minded and had some knowledge of the spirit world as strong psychic sense was present in her family. She was able to convince her young daughter that nothing was too strange, too weird, or too silly to say when it came to describing what she was so afraid of in her bedroom.

Then her daughter said, "I see two angels and they come and stand at my bedroom door and wake me up. They talk to me but I can't understand them. I hide under the blanket so they can't reach me."

When I heard this, I instantly knew Spirit was trying to communicate with this young girl. I began to reach out to the spirit communicators for more information and I was able to quickly link with one of the "angels" she was seeing—and this was her grandmother. (Her mother confirmed that the grandmother had passed away less than a year ago.) With grandmother was another family member in spirit that also wanted to say hello. The grandmother provided me with information and details that I gave to the mom for validation. There was no doubt; this was "Nana". It became clear that this grandmother in spirit was such a strong loving and "mama bear" grandmother that her energy was coming through just as strongly.

For a young child with no awareness that she is a sensitive medium, this can be a really scary event! To be overwhelmed by the energy of an excited grandmother in spirit and having your nervous system picking up on this energy without any prior exposure or understanding would also send me under the blankets in fear! (And of course, it did, as you now know.)

Once it was established who the spirit communicators were, I taught Mom and daughter the basics about what her daughter was experiencing energetically and why she felt like "they were coming closer" (spirit moving their energy closer and the aura sensing this). We talked about the aura and how some people are more sensitive to energies than others. We also talked about how to set some boundaries for her spirit family, such as asking them to not wake her up at night. In return, I suggested that the daughter and mother could acknowledge the spirits' presences and their wishes to communicate. The young girl had also done something before we met that told me her soul did have prior knowledge and experience and was trying to help. On her own, as she was getting into bed one night, she said loudly, "Please leave me alone tonight, I'm very tired." She was not awakened that night. She repeated this message for two nights, and both nights she was not awakened by her spirit visitors.

To help bring some perspective and to further disperse any lingering fears we also talked about all the unseen energies we know we can't see (with our physical eyes) like radio waves and microwaves. We even filmed some orbs in her room and she thought it was pretty interesting how they were all round and looked like bubbles. Explaining and providing examples of how sensitive she was to energies, moods and even animals really helped this young girl to understand that she was not under threat, nor was she weird. She was free to talk and ask questions about the subject .

Open discussion is so important when helping a young person overcome a fear of Spirit and of any unknown. Her mother and I were able tell this young daughter that as largely and loudly as her grandmother loved her when she was living, she was loving her as largely and loudly as she could from the spirit world now. This really made sense to her. She was in no danger, and although her grandmother's energy could be strong, we also told her she could ask "Nana" to step back and not be so forceful. These requests were honored by "Nana".

To let a child know they are perfectly normal when they are experiencing things many other children are not can seem kind of contradictory. The psychic senses and the spirit world are natural, and being sensitive or not sensitive to it are also natural. Every person is different, we will each experience these energies differently, or more, or less.

Intuition and empathic senses can overwhelm anyone if you have never had the exposure or opportunity to discover your natural talents. As children grow, they pass through many phases and stages of development on all levels. Their souls are always working to help them know themselves and to let their spirit shine through and express themselves. We can help them move through these phases with as little fear as possible, and grow compassion and understanding about themselves through all their experiences.

Development Tip

Think of spirits—deceased persons—as loved ones, people, rather than as ghostly apparitions or entities trying to frighten you. Spirit is more than willing to communicate with you on your terms if at all possible. If that means you are too afraid of what you will encounter or see day-to-day, then perhaps your spirit communication will take place only while you are sleeping and dreaming. If mediumship is your calling, it is to your benefit to identify, address and heal your fears so that you are able to be as clear a channel as possible for communicating with Spirit.

***

Our intuitive senses can grow and strengthen. For some, this happens all on its own without any direction or training. Typically, most people find that a structure like a workshop or course of study helps them focus so they too can succeed. I have benefitted greatly from the workshops and study I have completed. Exposure to different and new exercises from a variety of sources and teachers lets us learn and try out things. All this provides us with new experiences and knowledge. It also helps us find our own truths and certainties.

CHAPTER 13

Loving Signs from Spirit

The signs from the spirit world can be subtle and can be grand. Because every sign requires an energetic effort, the spirit world attempts to use the easiest and most efficient means of providing us a sign.

Sometimes it's a feather that lands in your path or on your shoulder and sometimes it's a blinking lamp light. "Pennies from heaven" are just that—an announcement, because Spirit does leave pennies and other coins for us to find. Coins are small objects that require less energy to manipulate.

It's been said that a person new to the spirit world, a recently deceased person, will need some time to adjust to their new surroundings. Perhaps they need some healing time or they themselves are not quite ready to get busy with life on the other side. In my experiences I have found that the level and skill of communication is different for each person that has crossed over. I never expect nor assume that a loved one in spirit is or is not going to jump in and communicate. Spirit will do as it is able and as it deems is the right thing to be done, and with whom.

Until I experienced first-hand the ability of spirit to manipulate objects, it was hard for me to really believe that it was all possible. The first time I participated in "table tipping", I was most amazed that a twenty-pound table could feel like a solid object one minute, and then feel weightless and lift off the floor. The science geek in me wanted to know more about how this was accomplished by the spirit world. Before I delved into how ectoplasm is used by Spirit, I examined some of the photographs I had taken of that table-tipping night. What I saw was even more exciting—I could see many small orbs clustered around and under the feet of the table as well as throughout the room. AHA! Based on the number of orbs, there were a lot of people in spirit helping out that night. The number of spirit helpers, and their efforts, were evident to me simply by seeing them in the photo.

Signs that are more subtle are just as important. Our spiritual family and helpers really want to know they have reached us. Some are better at big signs, most are good at the small signs and synchronicities. Sometimes a sign is seen right after a conversation and we say, "I was just talking about that..." At other times, our dreams become the focus for connection, especially if we are leading very busy lives with no down time or spare moments. Some of these subtle signs are:

+ Body chills or cool breezes

+ A strong emotional wave such as a "bliss bomb" or "love hug"

+ Pressure on the body—a hand on your shoulder, a stroke of your hair

+ Pets barking or wagging tails at empty space or at the ceiling

+ Songs in your head, or on the radio

+ Scents and smells (such as pipe smoke, perfume)

+ Hearing someone call your name

+ Objects being moved from one place to another, or disappearing and reappearing somewhere else

+ Pictures of your loved one falling for no reason; this tends to frighten people but it's not a bad sign— perhaps it was important to get your attention

Despite all the remarkable things that I have experienced, I feel just as amazed when my thoughts drift to someone I have lost, and next thing I see is a white feather floating down in front of me. That is the touch of Spirit—subtle, gentle and so full of love. Our loved ones will always find a way to let us know they are with us even if our days are crowded with tasks and events. And sometimes that sign arrives like a bull in a china shop.

A friend of mine told me a funny story about the message her husband received from his father in spirit. That morning, Mitch had just finished a shower in the upstairs bathroom. His life had become very stressful lately, and he knew he had been acting foolishly. As he stood in front of the small bathroom mirror he thought, "Dad, I could really use your help right now." The next moment a small plant hanging from the ceiling landed squarely on Mitch's head. He jumped in shock and started to swear—and then he laughed. He knew, without a doubt, that his father had heard and answered him with a familiar "knock some sense into yourself" message. Mitch did not suffer any injury, but he did have to clean up the scattered soil and hop back in the shower.

Spirit Loves Electricity

I am always learning about the capability of spirit to utilize energy. People have known for many years that spirit uses electricity and electrical devices such as lamps, telephones, and televisions to send signs.

I am quite sensitive to the presence and "chatter" of Spirit. When I am working with a client and his or her loved ones are excited, or there are many spirit communicators in the room, I do sense and hear the "crowd". On this particular night I was awakened around

2 a.m. with the sense that there was a lot of "chatter" taking place in my bedroom. It was like a crowd had arrived. As I have written about previously, I do have that contract so Spirit does not wake me up while I am sleeping, but this was different. Think of it as if you are trying to be quiet and not wake me up, but there are so many of you trying to be quiet and "hushing" each other that you wake me up anyway. As I lay there I knew there was a tremendous amount of traffic in my bedroom. As mentioned earlier, I had started filming orbs in my home after I learned how easy it was to do so I decided to turn on my phone video camera and see if I was correct. My camera showed hundreds of orbs streaming in and through my bedroom, in and out and back around. But what was most interesting was that they were all "young people" politely getting my attention. The collective message spirit was sending to me was that a young person was going to be joining them.

Since I was already awake, I got out of bed and walked into the dining room and stopped. Hmm, the ceiling fan was turned on, but I didn't do it and no one else was around. Did all that spirit activity turn it on? I thought it was interesting but really didn't give it much more thought. I thanked those in spirit for bringing me the message and wondered how I was connected to the person. My bed was calling me and the activity quieted, so I went back to sleep.

I was awakened again the next night at 3 a.m. My bedroom door faces the dining area, where the ceiling fan is located, and I don't close the door all the way. This time, the fan **and** the light were on.

I said to myself, "Ok, two nights in a row, someone in spirit is trying to get my attention. Or I have an electrical problem with the fan."

I shut off the fan and its light, acknowledging to Spirit that they had my attention, and back to bed I went.

The next day, I learned that on the previous night my friend Jenny's young daughter Courtney had died suddenly. Oh my, I thought, this is why the children in spirit had filled up my bedroom. They wanted to let me know they were expecting her, and, that she was not alone. Three days later, Jenny's daughter showed me that she was smartly working from her new home in spirit and seemed to be an expert at using my ceiling fan!

Over the next few months, this young spirit began using my ceiling fan about twice a week to communicate messages and connect with her mother, through me as the medium. It took me a few weeks at first to learn how she was using each setting on the fan for different meanings. This might sound pretty farfetched but you **can** communicate with spirit communicators and they will respond. You see this all the time on those ghost-hunter shows where the hosts ask a spirit to light up their electronic devices: different colored lights mean yes or no.

This is exactly how I sorted out what the meanings were for the fan light turning on, the fan running at low speed, and at high speed. Courtney's clear communication and understanding was shown when one evening I was lounging on the sofa watching television and the fan turned on at low speed. I said "Hello Courtney". Low speed was her signal to me that she was saying hello to her mother. So I would send Jenny a message and let her know her daughter had stopped by to say hello. Jenny always asks if there is a message to go along with that hello, but because it was almost 10p.m. and I was tired I told Jenny I would ask Courtney to turn on the fan light if she really wanted me to do a proper link and sitting for her. Within 10 minutes the fan light turned on. So we had a proper session although a bit late in the evening, and Jenny was able to hear from her daughter on many topics.

It truly was an amazing level of communication with a very smart young lady newly arrived in the spirit world. As heartbreaking as it is to have lost such a bright young person so suddenly, she certainly let it be known that she was as determined, funny and strong in spirit as she ever was in life.

The spirit world is masterful at lining up those people that are meant to be in our lives. I stopped asking why I was meeting this person or that person or why I ended up somewhere that was not in my plans. It has happened so often that I no longer try to figure out the synchronicities. I know that the reason I am in someone's life or periphery will be revealed when the time is right.

I met Jenny a few years before her daughter passed, when I had returned to school to study for my diploma in counseling. All I knew was that I felt it was important to keep in touch with Jenny after we had graduated, even if it was only once a year. I knew that we were brought together for a reason, but it only became clear when Jenny's family suffered the loss of their daughter, and Courtney decided to communicate with me. In the spirit world, Courtney would have known that I was a medium, and that I knew her mother. Even though I did not tell Jenny about the visits I was having from her daughter until the time was right for Jenny, Courtney knew, as did all those youngsters in the spirit world, that I could be a bridge for her to reach out to her family. I am so honored to be tapped on the shoulder by the spirit world to help bring their love, messages and healing through.

***

My experience with Courtney showed me that children in spirit are very adept when utilizing our electric and electronic devices to communicate with us. A number of months after Courtney initially began communicating via my ceiling fan I was in a rather bad mood one night and I turned off the fan by flipping the master switch that turns off all the electrical items on that wall; the one that shuts off the television, stereo, recorder, lights, etc. At 3:00 a.m. I was awakened by my microwave running and beeping non-stop. When I got up to check out what was happening the microwave then stopped running but the beeping continued and the panel on the microwave was blinking the word "SENSE". Nothing I did stopped the microwave from beeping and blinking so I unplugged it. I sheepishly apologized to Courtney for hitting the kill-switch on the ceiling fan. It was very clear to me that she was attempting to utilize other electronics to communicate for the next item affected was both my cell phones. The phones I was able to recover use of but the microwave never would work normally again. All it could do was beep and blink, "SENSE".

Although our loved ones can and will use our electrical/electronic items to communicate with us, I have asked the spirit communicators to take it easy on my appliances! Spirit does have a SENSE of humor....

CHAPTER 14

Into the Healing We Grow

No matter how you choose to use your intuitive skills, you still have to accept that patience, practice and dedication will be required on your part if you really want to find out your true potential. You must also be willing to do your own personal discovery and healing. There is no running away from your baggage so you might as well unpack it and sort it out. Then you can work on being the best person you can be, healing your wounds and developing your intuitive abilities at the same time.

By undertaking the study and development of your intuitive abilities, mediumship, healing and psychic senses, you can't help but reach into your soul and get to know everything there is to know about you—the spiritual being residing in your human body. Looking at the light within yourself also opens you up to really understand what others are going through. This awareness will bring compassion, love and connection when you assist others on their healing path, whether it's a vocation or just loving your friends and family. It's not a quest for perfection; it's a never-ending journey of discovery. Along the road you may find you have built a powerful relationship with the spirit world, your guides, angels and yourself.

Mediumship, as I have learned over decades of study, is not just about communicating with our loved ones beyond the veil. There are many forms to this healing vocation and it can be expressed through you via mental mediumship, physical mediumship, trance, spiritual healing, inspirational writing and speaking—just to name a few. The capacity we have to master these healing channels and natural abilities is unique to each person. For some, it is a grand and easy accomplishment. For others like me, it is a long and steady process of study and learning all about what makes you, you. All of the forms and expressions from the great healing Spirit are opportunities for healing others and ourselves.

You must be very certain that you are ready to work publicly or privately. Working with the public, and even just with family and friends, requires integrity, tact, discernment and of course, good listening skills, empathy and compassion. Joining a circle for the development of your mediumship is highly recommended. I didn't know the benefit until I joined one. It taught me new skills and it showed me what I had already gleaned from my own instincts, books, teachers, and by trying different things, training and, exploring.

There will always be the skeptic or stubborn client who sits across from me with arms crossed and tries to test, waiting for me to say the "code words" that they asked their loved one to say in their session. Since Spirit does not speak in code, and I receive only what that spirit communicator is able and wants to give, a skeptic may walk away believing me to be a failure. But I trust my spirit helpers so much that this kind of mindset from a client no longer upsets me. I know my spiritual helpers will provide what they can. It is this level of trust that I encourage you to find if you choose to pursue development in mediumship or in any spiritual and healing capacity.

I know that I may not be able to receive clearly every single time. I will always desire to be a clear channel but I know that there are things that can affect the process. Become aware of the personal biases or issues that stop you from working without ego. This will help you leave behind the need to be right or wrong or to convince others to believe in you.

My family in spirit, my guides and angels all have saved lives and protected those I love from harm. Until I experienced it for myself, and then for my family, I could only imagine how others experienced it. I suppose that was the weakest link in my belief system—*I* had to experience it to believe it possible. I did not know that my journey into mediumship could have been a lot easier if I had approached it with more trust in what I could not see, had not seen or experienced. But I did choose to learn by experience and that's what I got.

***

Now that my personal belief system has matured to the point where I know, believe, and accept that there is much more out there than I can presently comprehend or experience, the weight of having to prove everything to myself has lifted. I still believe that if I am going to share or teach anything to others that I must have personal experience with it. This does not mean that I have to have the ability, for example, to be a physical medium, but I have my experiences of it and my lessons from it and this I can share with others.

***

Until I experienced it for myself, I did not realize my soul was a traveller—a very old and wise spiritual being living in my human form. I was so young when I had my wakeup call from Spirit; I kept it to myself because I didn't know what to do with that knowledge. Now I do. How does the mind, with its thoughts, energy, love and intelligence of the spirit world continue to exist?

What is the science or universal law that makes it possible for us to live on after our physical body dies? At this point I don't have all the answers. But from all that I have seen and experienced, *everything* is possible.

CHAPTER 15

Be Brilliant

Perfection of one's ability, craft, talent or skill is great, but it's not very helpful when the pursuit of it creates blocks to the blossoming of one's true potential.

The following list includes suggestions and tips from my personal experiences and, from the mentors and teachers that I have met and studied with along the way. It's always a good thing to try out new ideas and tips for one of them may be the answer to something you are trying to learn or overcome. These tips are applicable at whatever stage you are at—from beginner to pro. These nuggets of wisdom have provided me with encouragement and perspective, and helped me go beyond the need for perfection, to enjoy blossoming at every step of my journey. These insights are helpful for anyone wishing to pursue the intuitive arts as a vocation or as a hobby. They also contain a few personal favorites that I apply to all areas of my life. The pursuit of perfection is probably a life-long quest for most mediums but this list isn't about being perfect. It's about letting the best *you* shine in all you do.

20 Tips for Brilliance

+ Make a commitment to yourself to do the very best you can.
+ Always work with, and keep, your integrity and honesty, and you will know you have done your best.
+ Believe in yourself as a part of something greater than you, and that you are an integral part of that.
+ Give up wishing and take up certainty with regard to your ability.
+ Some days your reception will be better than others; that's just the way it is.
+ Be dedicated to Spirit and yourself; don't let either down.
+ Be grateful for all that you have and are.
+ Find quiet meditation time every day to talk to Spirit, God, Higher self.
+ Give up and release all envy, jealousy and fear. It holds you back.

+ Not everyone will like you; get used to it and don't take it personally.

+ Don't try to please people when you are doing this work. Never try to make things fit. (Not everyone will like the guidance they receive.)

+ Trust what you are receiving. Don't ever analyze the message as it's coming through you will lose the link. Give what you receive—9 times out of 10 it is correct.

+ When giving a message or guidance use tact and discretion, be compassionate and caring.

+ Give credit to Spirit when it's due. You are just the messenger.

+ Become friends with your workers in spirit. Love, honor and respect them. However – do not put them on pedestal.

+ Learn to focus and stay focused.

+ Practice Practice Practice

+ Always take time to rest, relax and play frequently.

+ Always remember to cleanse your aura, ground and close off after your work or session.

+ Be at peace with yourself and your work. If you don't like the work, stop doing it.

Development Exercises

CHAPTER 16

Developing Your Personal Style
Exercise 1

I believe that one of the first things to learn when you begin to work on developing your psychic senses is how you receive your psychic or intuitive information, because this is personal to you. To start developing your psychic and intuitive abilities you need to know **how** you are receiving the information that flows to your physical body, nervous system and auric field. The **Self-Assessment Aura Exercise** will help you discover your individual style of receiving psychic information. It will also help you learn the commonly used terminology for your abilities: clairaudient, clairsentient, etc. There are instructions on how to do the exercise, followed by some information on how to interpret your results.

Some individuals are born with a natural awareness of their psychic or intuitive abilities. Others have a spiritual experience that provides them with what they need to know. For most people, figuring out how you are wired for receiving psychic details is rather like learning how to program your PVR with no instruction manual. It is, however, a worthwhile undertaking to learn about your abilities. As you understand more about your personal style, you will spend less time in confusion and doubt. You may try practicing the methods and styles of others but your blueprint is unique to you.

This exercise can be done any time throughout all stages of your development, for as your skills grow you will discover, or re-discover, something new about your own abilities and psychic methods of receiving. I have shared this exercise extensively in my workshops and it can provide you with valuable insight and knowledge about your intuitive senses. I still do this exercise and I always learn something new.

Preparation

This exercise does not require any preparation but it helps if you know something about **auras** and the **"clairs"** psychic senses. If you are a rank beginner and have no knowledge of the aura, then I suggest reading up on it before attempting this exercise.

Each person has a unique **aura** that is constantly filtering and absorbing, sending and receiving information and energy on many levels. The aura is what others sense as you approach them or walk into a room. In simpler terms, it is the energy bubble that surrounds you at all times. Your aura is constantly "on" and emitting its unique energy. Not everyone can see an aura with physical eyes, and that is not a failure or lack of any skill. Often when people begin to pursue metaphysical studies and healing modalities like Reiki, for example, their clairvoyant viewing (which takes place mostly in the mind's eye) begins to wake up and "see" what could not be seen with the physical eye. You may find that you naturally know more about the aura and energy than you think, but it is a good idea to have some knowledge on the subject. You can find helpful books on this and other subjects in the included bibliography.

**

The **"clairs"** psychic senses are the six extra-sensory perception senses that help us to sense energies beyond our five physical senses. The "clair" senses (originally French terms) referred to in the exercises are as follows:

CLAIRVOYANCE (CLEAR SEEING)

This is the intuitive sense that is most widely known for using the "third eye" or "mind's eye" to see beyond what our normal physical eyes could see. Visions and precognitive/futuristic views are in this category. Clairvoyant sight can be objective or subjective. Remote viewing techniques fall into this category.

CLAIRSENTIENCE (CLEAR FEELING)

This intuitive sense allows you to feel the emotions, physical wellness and pain of people, animals, spirit communicators, and places. Clairsentients sometimes feel another person's physical pain in their own body, as well as emotional pain. This is a key component of spirit communication and mediumship. An **empath** is clairsentient (a "sensitive") and reads and feels the emotions of other people and animals; in this way the empath is "feeling" your emotions. An empath can be affected by the mood of a crowd, or one person nearby, or a space that is imprinted with energy residue.

CLAIRCOGNIZANCE (CLEAR KNOWING)

This intuitive sense allows you to instantly know the details of anything or anyone (people, events, situations) without any prior knowledge. Instant knowing comes with a sense of certainty that the details received are accurate. Claircognizance is a knowing without hesitancy, as if, "The information just dropped in my brain out of nowhere" or "I suddenly just know it". It is often paired with a clairsentient feeling of emotion or "gut feeling" but it does not have to have any emotion attached to the information. It sometimes feels like a psychic "download" directly into the mind.

CLAIRGUSTANCE (CLEAR TASTE)

This intuitive sense allows you to taste an essence without putting anything in your mouth. The sensation of taste is often linked to/with an ethereal source such as a spirit communicator. For example, if the taste of chocolate builds as a spirit communicator draws closer, this psychic impression could be how that person identifies himself or herself. Perhaps he or she had a sweet tooth, loved chocolate or worked with chocolate.

CLAIRALIENCE (CLEAR SCENT)

Also known as clairessence or clairolfaction, this intuitive sense allows you to smell scents and aromas that are not physically present.   Aromas are often linked to/with an ethereal source such as a spirit communicator. For example, you may smell the perfume that a loved one in spirit used to wear, or you may smell smoke as a firefighter in spirit comes close.

CLAIRAUDIENCE (CLEAR HEARING)

This intuitive sense allows you to hear voices, sounds, words or music that are not physically present. These sounds are often linked to/with an ethereal source.

Psychics who are clairaudient receive these sounds mentally (the psychic inner hearing) or within their ears. There are some clairaudient psychics that will hear spirit voices loudly, and it may sound like someone is speaking directly beside one of their ears. Clairaudients also are known to hear songs or parts of songs in their minds. The source may be from either the spirit realms or can be received on the psychic airwaves. For example, if a song gets "stuck in your head" and it turns out your best friend has been listening to the same song all day, then you have psychically tuned in to your friend and "heard" the sounds.

***

Instructions for the Self-Assessment Aura Exercise

The self-assessment aura exercise can be done without a partner, but for beginners I recommend you do this with a partner, even someone you don't know very well. There are strict guidelines to follow in order to provide you with the best results. Read through the steps below **before** you start working on the questions. This is where you begin to TRUST yourself, the process and your ethereal helpers!

Note: Read through the steps below before you start working on the questions.

Supplies: Chair, pen and a question sheet for each participant.

Steps for the Exercise

With a partner, determine who will be the "client" and who will be the "reader".

Place a chair so that there is enough space for the reader to walk around it comfortably without touching the client (a 3–4 foot diameter around the chair is good).

Have the person designated as the client sit in the chair. The client must sit with eyes closed until the reader has completed the exercise. The reader will stand or walk around the client as needed. Refrain from talking during this exercise.

Reader: You can use your hands to sense the shape of the aura or energy but you cannot touch your partner (the client).

Client: You don't have to do anything but sit with your eyes closed and relax while your partner works through the questions.

You (the reader) will try to receive one impression, whatever it may be, for each question on the sheet. If nothing comes through, don't panic! If you have no image, word or feeling after 1–2 minutes, just move on to the next question. If you receive more than one impression, jot them down in point form as quickly as they arrive.

Note: Allow a maximum of two minutes for "sensing" per question. Any longer than that and your mind will start to chatter and interfere.

THIS IS THE MOST IMPORTANT PART OF THE EXERCISE:

Reader: You must write down your first impression as soon as it enters your thoughts; no hesitating, no questioning what you get, just write it down immediately. It does not matter how strange, silly, short or weird the information, image or feeling. Do not second-guess or analyze or judge the impression because this blocks the flow. Write down the impression as soon as it is received and then move on to the next question.

For example, for the question "What do I see?", if you suddenly get the image in your mind of a giant letter F when you gaze at your client's aura, then on your paper you write "giant letter F", and move to the next question if there are no other impressions coming through on that active question. Do not stop to review what you have written down! You will have the opportunity to review and assess your findings after both parties have completed the exercise.

Once the exercise is complete, the reader and the client switch places and the exercise is repeated. Remember, information will not be shared until both have finished the exercise.

Once both of you have completed the exercise, share your results. You will then be able to work with each other and interpret your findings. You will find guidelines for sharing and interpreting your results following the exercise sheet.

SELF-ASSESSMENT AURA EXERCISE WORKSHEET	
Reader: _____ Client: _____	
What do I feel?	
What do I hear?	
What do I smell?	
What do I taste?	
What do I know?	
Date: _____	

Share and Interpret Your Results

In order to have a full understanding of your experience, it is best to review this exercise with an experienced teacher or facilitator immediately after the exercise. If you are not in a workshop setting and cannot discuss your results with your instructor right away, I suggest you record the results from you and your partner using any kind of recording equipment you have on hand (such as your smartphone). You can share that recording later with your teacher for further detailed discussion, or keep it for your own review and as a record of your progress. If you are working with a partner and have no one to act as an instructor, continue on and share the exercise with each other as soon as you have completed it.

BEGIN BY SHARING YOUR IMPRESSIONS

For each question, take turns and read your impressions out loud to your client. As you do this, see if you can pay close attention to the words you are using as you describe your impression in more depth to your partner. This will help you to recognize any "clair" senses that you used. Your partner can help you too by listening to the words you choose to describe what you have sensed. For example:

Question: What do I know?

Impression Noted: *Feeling irritated.* I knew you were feeling impatient. I felt irritated all of a sudden.

Now let's look at that impression. Where did you receive that information in your body? Did it suddenly arrive in your mind, or did you suddenly feel like you had to move around? Maybe you felt a small jolt of irritation, too. If you look very closely at those words, you will see that the words used are actually describing:

Clairsentience: **Feeling** irritated

Claircognizance: I **knew** you were irritated at something.

Now let's dig a little deeper. What did that **feel** like in your body? **Where** did you feel irritated? Was it your legs or your stomach that felt something? What part of your body or mind gave you that piece of information? Did it suddenly appear in your mind? Did it arrive after you felt the emotion of irritation? As you can see from the example above, there may be one or two metaphysical senses at work.

We dig deeper into the words we use to describe what we are sensing because it helps split out the psychic information so that you know how it feels to **you**, when you receive it. You also start to know where information comes in and when it becomes second nature to you, you will know **why** it comes in that way. Here is another example:

Question: What did I hear?

Impression Noted: *Man's voice.* I heard a man's voice.

Question: What did I feel?

Impression Noted: *Love.* I felt pressure in my chest and I got teary-eyed.

Now let's dig a little deeper. When you heard a man's voice, (clairaudience), **where** did you hear the voice? Was it outside of your head or inside your mind? When you felt love (clairsentience), **where** did you feel it? Did it come with a temperature? A color? When you felt teary-eyed (clairsentience), what emotion were you feeling when you got teary-eyed? Where in your body did you feel that emotion? As you can see from this example, two psychic senses are at work: clairsentience and clairaudience.

When you are just beginning to learn about how you receive information, this kind of dissection of your psychic impressions may seem a bit overwhelming. I encourage you to take the time to delve deeper into even your shortest impression or intuitive "hits". This way you can get to know how your body/energy works to receive and decipher psychic and subtle energies. The next time you are aware that your intuition is picking up on something, stop and check in with yourself to see how and where it is coming to you. What "clair" sense is bringing you that sensation or information?

***

Don't forget to have fun with the exercise. Intuitive information flows easier when you are relaxed and heart-centered. Remember to cleanse your aura, ground and "close off" after your practice.

CHAPTER 17

How to Sense Your Guides, Angels and Spirit Helpers
Exercise 2

The **Sensing Exercise for All Levels** is perfect for any stage of your intuitive development. It will help you discover your individual way of sensing the differences between the energies, vibrations, thoughts and emotions of spirit guides, guardian angels and spirit people/deceased loved ones. Like us, they are all part of the same source; around the world they are known and called by many different names. They each have different energetic blueprints, especially if they are highly evolved or highly experienced. There are instructions on how to do the exercise, followed by some information on how to interpret your results.

I still do this exercise and I do it just because I want to send my helpers some love and express my gratitude to them. And on those days when I'm having a bit of a pity-party, it's nice to reconnect with their energies and lift out of my slump.

Preparation

Before you start this exercise, I want you to make an agreement with yourself. The agreement is that you will trust yourself, your senses and your spiritual helpers. If it is hard for you to let someone help you, then consider allowing yourself to be surprised by your spirit team. Rather than thinking you are vulnerable, consider yourself a student about to learn something new.

Before I begin any practice or work sessions, I always say a prayer and bless the room or space I am working in. Sometimes I smudge or clear the space if I deem that is necessary. I set my intention to work for the highest good with the highest energies. I also thank all of my helpers in advance. That is my personal ritual.

Whatever blessing or ritual you may or may not incorporate, I highly recommend setting the intention of your practice to be for the highest good and setting the space to be filled with the highest vibration.

You don't need a partner or an instructor for the sensing exercise. Read the instructions through and, if you wish, record the instructions so you can play them back for yourself to follow along as you sit and connect with the energies. Your spirit team, angels and guides all want to help you — so let them help you.

***

Instructions for the Sensing Exercise for All Levels

Note: Read through the steps below before you start.

Find a comfortable quiet place to sit where you will have 10 to 15 minutes undisturbed. This exercise is best done indoors at first, especially if you have not done it before. It can be done outdoors if you are used to ignoring other distractions and stimulation from your environment. But if the wind is wildly whipping your hair, you may have difficulty tuning in to the subtle energies of the guides and spirit communicators.

Steps for the Exercise

Sit comfortably upright with your feet on the floor; let your hands rest on your lap (or on the arms of the chair).

Close your eyes and take a few relaxing breaths. As you breathe, release any tension or hustle-bustle energy that may be running through you.

Now you are breathing calmly; quiet your mind so that you feel relaxed and open.

When you are ready, invite your spirit team, guides and angels to be with you. You can do this by saying:

"I invite and ask my angels, guides and spirit helpers to be here now to help me with this experiment."

You will repeat the next set of instructions three times as you work with your spirit guide, your guardian angel and a loved one in spirit.

SPIRIT GUIDE

When you are ready, ask your **spirit guide** to bring their energy very close to you by saying:

"I ask my spirit guide to come and stand beside me and bring your energy close to me."

This is the most important part: You don't have to <u>do</u> anything but sit quietly with your eyes closed. (If you find it difficult to sit with closed eyes, keep them open and let your gaze be relaxed and unfocused—staring at the floor works great.)

Let yourself be aware of any subtle changes close to your body, within your aura or nearby. This could be a feeling of warmth, a sensation of pressure, a strong emotion, or something else. You may get a sense of masculine or feminine energy. Take a mental note of where you feel sensations on your body, on your back, left side, right side, or some other spot. If you sense a connection—say hello or even "I can feel/sense you", to let your guide know you are aware of their presence.

If you feel nothing at all, repeat your request, asking your guide to step **even closer** to you so that you may be aware of your guide's presence and energy. Give your guide a moment or two to do as you have requested. Even if you are not sensing or feeling anything, know that your guide is there and is working to find the best way to connect with you.

Now ask your spirit guide to step back and withdraw their energy by saying:

"Thank you, would you now step back and withdraw your energy".

Be aware of any shifts you may sense as your guide withdraws this energy.

GUARDIAN ANGEL

Next you are going to ask your **guardian angel** to bring their energy very close to you by saying:

"I ask that my guardian angel come and stand beside me and bring your energy close to me."

As before, sit quietly with your eyes closed. Let yourself be aware of any subtle changes close to your body, within your aura or nearby. This could be a feeling of warmth, a sensation of pressure, a strong emotion, or something else. Take a mental note of where you feel this on your body, on your back, left side, right side, or some other spot. As before, if you sense a connection—do say hello or even "I can feel/sense you", to let your angel know you are aware of their presence.

If you feel nothing at all, repeat your request, asking your guardian angel to step **even closer** to you, to blend more with your aura. Give your guardian angel a moment or two to do as you have requested. Even if you are not sensing or feeling anything, know that your guardian angel is there and is working to find the best way to connect with you.

Now ask your guardian angel to step back and withdraw their energy by saying:

"Thank you, would you now step back and withdraw your energy".

Be aware of any shifts you may sense as your guardian angel withdraws this energy.

Loved One in Spirit

Next you will Ask a **loved one in spirit** to bring their energy very close to you by saying:

"I ask that a loved one in spirit who is strongest and most able to come forward, to come and stand beside me and bring your energy close to me."

By asking for the strongest communicator to step forward it helps the spirit world send forward the one most able to step forward. It may not be the person you expect or hope will come forward and, you may not know who it is, but Spirit will do all they can to help you sense their energy.

As before, sit quietly with your eyes closed. Let yourself be aware of any subtle changes close to your body, within your aura or nearby. This could be a feeling of warmth, a sensation of pressure, a strong emotion, or something else. Take a mental note of where you feel this on your body, on your back, left side, right side, or some other spot.

If you feel nothing at all, repeat your request, asking your spirit communicator to step **even closer** to you, to blend more with your aura. Give the spirit communicator a moment or two to do as you have requested. Even if you are not sensing or feeling anything, know that your loved one is there and is working to find the best way to connect with you.

Now ask your loved one in spirit to step back and withdraw their energy by saying:

"Thank you, would you now step back and withdraw your energy".

Be aware of any shifts you may sense as your loved one in spirit withdraws their energy.

Next, Ask once again for your **guardian angel** to step forward and bring their energy close to you. See if you notice any shift in sensations, energy, temperature or emotions. Ask your guardian angel to step back and withdraw their energy.

Next, ask your **spirit guide** to step forward and this time stand on your *right* side. See if you notice any shift in sensations, energy, temperature or emotions.

Next, ask your **spirit guide** to now move and stand by your *left* side. Once again, see if you notice any shift in sensations, energy, temperature or emotions. Then, ask your spirit guide to step back and withdraw their energy.

Lastly, tell everyone that the exercise is now completed and ask them to withdraw their energies. When you feel that the energy has shifted, offer your thanks and gratitude to your spirit guide, guardian angels and loved ones is spirit. They do notice and appreciate your gratitude and your thanks.

Interpret Your Results

If you have never done an exercise like this before please know that it is not unusual if you don't sense anything the first time through. Also, it's common for new students to sense one presence, but not another. If this happens remember it is not failure—you and your spirit team are learning how to work together.

If you have had **no** success in sensing any energies or energy shifts with this experiment, don't be discouraged! Sensing is just like exercising a muscle, and with practice you will fine-tune all of your senses and your "antenna". If it does not work the first time you try it, don't give up! Set aside some time to try again.

***

Here is a list of some of the ways you may feel, sense, or know the presence of spiritual helpers:

+ Tingling beginning at feet and moving upward or tingling moving down legs
+ Cool breeze across lower legs, or neck and shoulder area
+ Sudden heat in the heart chakra area or brow/third eye
+ Buzzing, ringing, burning or fluttering sensation in ears

- ✦ Pressure on the back or top of head/crown chakra that may increase in strength

- ✦ Full body heat, either sudden or a wave, or full body chills or goose bumps

- ✦ Feeling/sensing pressure (light or strong) or a cool breeze on one side of body

- ✦ Temperature drop in the room

- ✦ A rush of emotion: tears, joy, love, connection, bliss

- ✦ Feeling a wave of energy rolling across you, come from behind you, or rippling through you

- ✦ Sudden racing heartbeat (not from nervousness or anxiety)

- ✦ Sensing/feeling like the sun or a very bright light is beaming on your eyes and face (with eyes closed)

- ✦ Suddenly "knowing" who is with you—instant knowledge

***

The experiences listed above are actual responses from many people. Your sensations and experiences will be unique to you. Learning to sense differences in energies is an important part of development. For some it comes easily and for others not so quickly; this is for a wide variety of reasons. If you are having a rough day, your sensing antenna might not be at full capacity or alternatively, you could be so mellow and relaxed that you would rather be sleeping! Like a fine instrument, we must learn to tune and hone all of our abilities.

You can repeat this exercise whenever you wish. If you feel that you are not making any progress in sensing, I suggest you try to do the exercise once a day, when you are not too tired and can have the time to enjoy practicing.

***

My Exercise Notes

My Experiences

This page is for you to jot down your personal experiences with all things Spirit

.

About the Author

Leanda Rae is an internationally known medium, clairvoyant, spiritual teacher and mentor providing both private and group sessions, public galleries and workshops.

With over twenty-five years experience, Leanda has touched many souls and hearts through her work as a psychic, medium and healer whether in a personal sitting, public demonstration, or attending one of her exceptional workshops. She has appeared on radio and at various festivals, and has been speaker and tutor at the Edgar Cayce A.R.E. Summer Retreat and the Seabeck Mediumship Retreat in WA.

Leanda holds a Diploma of Professional Counselling, is a Reiki Master/Teacher, Angel Therapy Practitioner®, has studied mediumship at the world-renowned Arthur Findlay College, and with many other private tutors. She has studied with top mediums and healing practitioners from North America and Europe. She works with clientele around the world and is based in the Vancouver, Canada region.

For more information visit www.spiritsay.com

Bibliography & Suggested Reading

All About Mediumship, Ursula Roberts. Two Worlds. 1994

Angel Therapy, Doreen Virtue. Hay House. 1997

Archangels & Ascended Masters, Doreen Virtue. Hay House. 2004

Ask and it is Given: Learning to Manifest Your Desires, Esther and Jerry Hicks. Hay House. 2005

Auras, Edgar Cayce. A.R.E. Press. 1989

Clearing : A Guide to Liberating Energies Trapped in Buildings and Lands, Jim PathFinder Ewing. Findhorn Press. 2006

Conversations with God: An Uncommon Dialogue Book 1, Neale Donald Walsch. G. P. Putnam's Sons. 1995

Crossing Over, John Edward, Jodere Group. 2001

Divine Prescriptions: Spiritual Solutions for You and Your Loved Ones, Doreen Virtue. Hay House 2011.

Essential Reiki: A Complete Guide to an Ancient Healing Art, Diane Stein. Crossing Press. 1995

Genuine Mediumship, Swami Bhakta Vishita. Yoga Publication Society. 1919

Hands of Light: A Guide to Healing Through the Human Energy Field, Barbara Brennan. Bantam. 1988

Healing with the Fairies, Doreen Virtue. Hay House. 2001

How to Meet and Work with Spirit Guides, Ted Andrews. Llewellyn Worldwide. 2011

How to See and Read the Aura, Ted Andrews. Llewellyn Worldwide. 2006

Light from Silver Birch, compiled by Pam Riva, 1983/2009. Spiritual Truth Press

MAP: The Co-Creative White Brotherhood Medical Assistance Program, Perelandra Ltd, 1994.

Messengers of Light, Terry Lynn Taylor. H.J Kramer Publishing. 1993

Messages from your Angels, Doreen Virtue. Hay House. 2002

Opening to Channel: How to Connect with Your Guide, Sanaya Roman. H.J. Kramer Publishing. 1993

Personal Power Through Awareness: A Guidebook for Sensitive People, Sanaya Roman. H.J. Kramer Publishing. 1993

Psychic Healing with Spirit Guides and Angels, Diane Stein. Ten Speed Press, 1996

Secrets of a Medium, Larry Dreller. Red Wheel/Weiser Books. 2003

Spirit Healing, Harry Edwards. The Harry Edwards Spiritual Healing Sanctuary Trust. 1960/1993

Teachings of Silver Birch, A.W. Austen, 1938/2010. Spiritual Truth Press

The Encyclopedia of Angels, Rosemary Ellen Guiley. Facts On File. 1996

The Lightworker's Way, Doreen Virtue. Hay House. 1997

World Wide Web (www.)

www.ingramcontent.com/pod-product-compliance
Lightning Source LLC
LaVergne TN
LVHW051122080426
835510LV00018B/2188